ANSWERING
BIBLE
DIFFICULTIES

THERE ARE NO
ERRORS IN THE
BIBLE

DON STEWART

Answering Bible Difficulties:
There Are No Errors In The Bible

TABLE OF CONTENTS

INTRODUCTION

The Bible is God's trustworthy revelation of Himself to humanity. Historically, Christians have believed that His Word is true in all that it teaches. However, believers do recognize that the Bible does contain a number of difficulties. This book concerns the subject of Bible difficulties as well as the doctrine of the inerrancy, or trustworthiness, of Scripture.

Inerrancy is a theological term that is used by a number of Christians to explain the nature of the Bible—it is without error. Yet, not everyone is convinced of this.

So many questions are raised by believers and unbelievers alike. Does the Bible contain any errors in its contents? Are there mistakes and contradictions in the original text of Scripture? Can a holy God divinely inspire a Book that contains errors? Does it really matter, one way or another, if there are errors in Scripture? These and other similar issues will be considered as we examine this very important topic.

We will also look at a number of specific objections that are often raised against the idea of an inerrant Bible. It will be seen that all of these objections have reasonable answers. When all the evidence is in, it will be found that the Bible is exactly what it claims to be; God's error-free Word, totally trustworthy in all that it teaches.

What Is The Doctrine Of Biblical Inerrancy?

One of the terms used in describing the nature of the Bible is "inerrancy." While inerrancy is not a biblical term, but rather a theological term, it does express a biblical truth. In fact, there are a number of theological terms that are not found in Scripture which believers have used for centuries.

An example of this is the word "Trinity." Trinity is not a biblical term, but it sums up what the Bible has to say about the nature of God. In the same manner, inerrancy sums up the truth about what the Bible has to say about itself—it is without error.

A number of important points need to be made about the doctrine of biblical inerrancy. They include the following.

INERRANCY IS A RELATIVELY NEW TERM BUT A CLEAR BIBLICAL CONCEPT

While inerrancy is a new term, coined within the last one hundred years, it describes a concept that the Bible clearly teaches about itself and that the church has held from the beginning—God's Word is without error.

Over time, the terminology in describing the nature of the Bible has changed. The term inerrancy came into common usage as a response to those who claimed to have found errors in Scripture. It was merely expressing the concept of God's truthfulness in a way that responded to the charges that were made against it.

Therefore, the fact that the precise term "inerrancy" is not found in Scripture, in the historic creeds, or in confessional statements, is not relevant. Historically the church has built all its doctrines out of the teachings found in Scripture which has been believed to be authoritative and completely truthful in all that it teaches.

Consequently, the real issue is not about the term "inerrancy"—the real issue is this: Is the Bible totally trustworthy in all that it says. It is the concept that is important, not the particular term that is used to describe the concept.

THE DOCTRINE OF INERRANCY DRAWS A LINE BETWEEN PROFESSING CHRISTIANS

The concept of inerrancy has become a divisive issue among those who profess to be Christians. Those who place their trust in their own powers of reasoning and their ability to critically judge the Scripture reject the doctrine of inerrancy.

Unfortunately, a number of Bible-believing Christians have fallen into this trap. While still professing faith in the God of the Bible they also claim that His Word contains errors.

On the other hand, those who submit to the authority of Scripture have no problem in acknowledging the doctrine of inerrancy. While they do not have explanations for every difficulty, they have faith that the ultimate author of Scripture, God, has given the human race a revelation of Himself that is consistent with His character, and thus it is error-free.

SOME BELIEVERS HAVE MADE CARELESS STATEMENTS IN DEFENDING INERRANCY

There is something else that has to be mentioned. Those who defend inerrancy admit that not all defenders of the doctrine have done this in a clear and reasoned manner.

Examples can be given of overzealous believers who have made careless statements in an attempt to preserve this doctrine. In their desire to defend the inerrancy of Scripture they have opened themselves up to criticism and ridicule.

Indeed, some people have attempted to make the Scripture much more precise than it intends to be. They attempt to insist that every statement is meant to be scientifically precise or exact.

However, this is not the case. There are a number of places in Scripture where the language is meant to be imprecise or ambiguous. We should always allow the context to determine whether the writer is speaking in generalities or is trying to be precise. Let us not make the Bible say more than it is attempting to say.

Others, in an attempt to defend inerrancy, have denied such legitimate disciplines as textual criticism. Textual criticism is a legitimate field of study which attempts to recover the original text of Scripture. It is wrong to say that such a quest is unnecessary. By saying things like this, it gives the impression that Christians who believe in the inerrancy of Scripture refuse to face difficult issues which arise. This is certainly not the case.

There are still others who have claimed that inerrancy is a direct teaching of the Bible rather than acknowledging that it is the logical implication of what the Bible says about itself. Again, this is saying more than the Bible says.

All of these shortcomings are irrelevant to the issue as to whether the doctrine of inerrancy is, or is not, true. The fact that some misuse the term is not the real issue. The correctness of the doctrine has to be decided from a consideration of what the Scripture says about itself and whether or not the evidence supports the biblical claim. It is simply not true that the belief in inerrancy naturally leads to erroneous views of interpreting Scripture.

THE ETERNAL SALVATION OF A PERSON IS NOT DETERMINED UPON THEIR VIEW OF INERRANCY

While inerrancy is an important belief, the eternal salvation of an individual is not dependent upon a person's view of the subject. That is determined solely upon one's relationship with Jesus Christ. However, inerrancy is an essential foundational concept and its importance should not be minimized.

THE DOCTRINE OF INERRANCY DEFINED

Inerrancy, or infallibility, means that when all the facts are known, the Bible, in the original autographs, when properly interpreted, will prove itself to be without error in all matters that it covers. These include areas of theology, history, science, and all other disciplines of knowledge—they will be in perfect accord with the truth. The Bible, therefore, is totally trustworthy in everything that it records or teaches.

THE DEFINITION OF INERRANCY EXPANDED

We will now expand this definition of inerrancy. The following observations need to be made about what we mean by the doctrine of inerrancy.

1. WHEN ALL THE FACTS ARE KNOWN THE BIBLE IS INERRANT

First, we emphasize that the Bible will prove itself inerrant when all the facts are known. As finite human beings we do not know all the facts. This is where faith must come in.

Hence, it is wrong to accuse the Scripture of being in error in a certain place when our knowledge may be limited. Ultimately, the Bible will prove itself to be true. Time and time again the Bible has proven to be accurate in places where it was formerly suspected of inaccuracy. Therefore, in areas of difficulty we wait for further information to solve the problems.

2. THE BIBLE IS INERRANT ONLY IN THE ORIGINAL WRITINGS

Inerrancy only deals with the original writings of the authors of Scripture. There is no claim that the various copies of the manuscripts made throughout the years are inerrant. Neither is there any claim that any one translation of the Bible is inerrant.

However, this is not to say that the manuscript copies we presently have are corrupt, or that we cannot trust recent translations of the Bible (such as the *English Standard Version, The New International Version*, and the *New English Translation*).

To the contrary, these and other modern translations are based upon a solid textual foundation. Furthermore, the message is loud and clear. Therefore, the inerrancy of Scripture comes through in the modern translations.

SOME LATER EDITING MAY HAVE OCCURRED

It is likely that later writers of Scripture possibly edited some of the earlier writings, such as the five books of Moses. If this is the case, then the editing by these prophets would have also been under the direct guidance of the Holy Spirit.

Therefore, when we say that only the originals were without error this would include any later additions, or editing, to a particular biblical book which was done during the biblical period.

We limit any editing to the biblical period because there were only limited times in history in which God divinely inspired the writing of Holy Scripture—this was not something which was happening constantly.

IT IS THE WRITINGS, NOT THE WRITERS

This brings us to another important point. Inerrancy extends to the writings of the different authors, not to the writers themselves. It is the finished product that is error-free, not the individuals who wrote the documents. The Bible says:

> All Scripture is breathed out by God and profitable for teaching, for reproof, for correction, and for training in righteousness, that the man of God may be competent, equipped for every good work (2 Timothy 3:16,17 ESV).

It is the Scripture, the final product, that is God-breathed, not the writers themselves.

3. THE BIBLE IS INERRANT ONLY WHEN IT IS PROPERLY INTERPRETED

This point emphasizes that Scripture is inerrant insofar as the Bible is properly interpreted. Proper interpretation consists of asking, at least, the following questions.

First, we want to know the identity of the human author and the identity of the audience to whom he was writing.

Next, we want to know the occasion or purpose for the author writing this work—why was it composed?

Then we ask, what was the background (both cultural and historical) of the people or the individual to which he wrote? The truth of Scripture is expressed accurately within accepted cultural norms when it was written.

We also want to know what the words mean in context, in their original language, to the people, or to the individual, to whom the document was written at that particular time in history.

It is also important to discover how precise the author is attempting to be in what he says. What is the text intending to teach? Is the author speaking in approximations, or is he trying to be precise?

Matters of precision and accuracy are to be determined in light of ancient standards in the culture where the document was written, not by modern standards. These standards of precision should apply when determining whether or not an author is in error.

These issues must be taken into consideration when attempting to interpret the Scripture.

4. THE BIBLE IS WITHOUT ERROR OR COMPLETELY TRUE IN ALL AREAS IN WHICH IT SPEAKS

When we say the Bible is without error, or completely true in all that it says, we mean there are no statements in the Bible which are falsely reported and no teachings which are inaccurate. Every statement, every event, is recorded for us truthfully. There are no deceptions or inaccuracies, whether willful or unwilful, in the pages of Scripture.

This, however, does not mean that every statement found in the Bible is true. For example, every time the devil spoke, he lied. Yet the lies that he uttered are accurately recorded in Scripture. The real issue is truthfulness, and the Bible tells the truth in all that it says and teaches.

This last point emphasizes that inerrancy extends to all areas in which it speaks. The Bible makes no distinction between religious matters and non-religious matters. Truth is truth—whether it is spiritual truth or other kinds of truth.

All matters in Scripture are dealt with in a truthful, or an error-free way. This includes areas of history, science, and geography as well as theology. Issues of science and history, however, must be evaluated in light of the intention of the author, and the degree of precision he is attempting to use. It is unfair to make the writers of Scripture conform to modern standards of scientific precision and historical writing.

Also, in areas of science, we must be careful not to make the biblical writers say more than they are attempting to say. On the other hand, we should not make them say less than what they wanted to say. Again, the key is to discover what they were trying to say, and the degree of precision they were trying to say it with.

BEYOND THE TERM INERRANCY: THE BIBLE IS TOTALLY TRUSTWORTHY

While it is important to believe and teach that the Bible is inerrant in the statements that it makes, we must realize that the term inerrancy is not sufficient in-and-of itself.

Inerrancy does not explain all the data we find in Scripture. The Bible is more than a number of true assertions or statements that God has given to humanity.

Indeed, Scripture contains statements of worship, ethical commands, and statements of God's faithfulness.

While these statements are true, they cannot be verified in the same way that we can verify historical statements such as Pontius Pilate was the Governor, or Prefect, of Judea, or that Jerusalem was destroyed by the Babylonians about six hundred years before the time of Christ.

In addition, inerrancy is a negative term. It says there are no errors in Scripture. However, this is not saying enough about the nature of Scripture.

Therefore, we must go beyond the term inerrancy and say that everything recorded in the Bible is totally trustworthy. This includes parts that cannot be verified.

In other words, Scripture is true in all that it says, not just the historical facts. Consequently, when we use the word "inerrant" when discussing the nature of Scripture, we must realize that what we are ultimately saying is that the Bible is absolutely trustworthy in all that it records.

SUMMARY TO QUESTION 1
WHAT IS THE DOCTRINE OF BIBLICAL INERRANCY?

The doctrine of inerrancy teaches that the Bible, when properly interpreted, does not make any mistakes, or contain any legends, or myths. In other words, there are not any mistakes in recording historical events, or stating theological truths. The Bible is not deceitful or fraudulent in any way.

This is only true in the original autographs of Scripture—not copies or translations.

Inerrancy extends to areas of theology, history, science, and all other disciplines of knowledge. Consequently, everything written in Scripture can be trusted as being recorded accurately.

It is simply not true as some have contended that the belief in inerrancy naturally leads to erroneous views of interpreting Scripture.

However, the term inerrancy is somewhat limited for there are many statements in the Bible that cannot be categorized as errant or inerrant. What needs to be emphasized is that these statements are totally trustworthy in all that they say.

Therefore, when we use the term inerrant, the emphasis should be on the total trustworthiness of Scripture.

QUESTION 2

What Are Some Important Clarifications To The Doctrine Of Inerrancy?

In order to have a proper understanding of what the Bible says about itself, there are a number of important clarifications that need to be made to the doctrine of the inerrancy, or the trustworthiness of Scripture. They include the following.

1. THE BIBLE IS INERRANT WHEN CONFORMING TO ANCIENT STANDARDS OF HISTORICAL ACCURACY

This point is essential. Scripture was written in the ancient world to ancient peoples. Therefore, the writers should not be required to write like modern-day historical writers. This does not mean that the writers of Scripture were inaccurate—it means that they wrote in an inerrant way according to the standards current at the time.

For example, there is no attempt to fill in all the major historical details of the history of the descendants of Abraham. Indeed, we find that in the first few verses in the Book of Exodus several centuries are covered:

> All those who were descendants of Jacob were seventy persons (for Joseph was in Egypt *already*). And Joseph died, all his brothers, and all that generation. But the children of Israel were fruitful and increased abundantly, multiplied and

grew exceedingly mighty; and the land was filled with them. Now there arose a new king over Egypt, who did not know Joseph (Exodus 1:5-8 NKJV).

Therefore, we should never attempt to make the writers of Scripture something that it was impossible for them to be—modern historical writers.

2. INERRANCY ALLOWS FOR NON-TECHNICAL DESCRIPTIONS

The doctrine of inerrancy allows for the Bible to be written in non-technical descriptions. We must allow for a biblical writer to explain a natural event from the point of view of an observer. An example of this is that the Bible says that "dew fell:"

> And when the dew fell on the camp in the night, the manna fell on it. (Numbers 11:9 NKJV).

Dew does not literally fall down. This statement, although not scientifically precise, is exactly what it looks like from the vantage point of an observer.

We do not need to assume the writer is making a scientific statement about the nature of the universe when such a statement is made. Inerrancy allows for these types of statements. The Bible was written in the common, non-technical language of its day. It was not written in scientific language, or unscientific language, rather it was written in *non-scientific* language.

3. INERRANCY ALLOWS FOR PICTORIAL LANGUAGE

Holding to an inerrant Bible allows for pictorial language and figures of speech. Interpreting the Bible literally does not rule out figurative language when the context calls for it. The Bible uses literary devices such as metaphor, simile, and hyperbole to make a point. Truth can be communicated through figures of speech.

Inerrancy, therefore, does not mean that passages need to be interpreted in a "wooden literal" manner—it does recognize figures of speech when the context calls for it.

4. INERRANCY DOES NOT DEMAND EXACT PRECISION

Inerrancy means that a statement can be true without scientific precision. General statements can be inerrant without being precise if the writer and the readers understood that exact precision was not intended. This is best illustrated in the practice of Scripture of rounding off the numbers. We find this happening often in Scripture.

5. INERRANCY ALLOWS FOR RECORDING DIFFERENT DETAILS OF THE SAME EVENTS

The doctrine of inerrancy also allows for different writers to describe the same events with different details. This is particularly the case with the four gospels.

Each gospel writer would have viewed events from his own unique perspective. This would account for the reason that some of the details appear different. The Gospels record many of the same events with explanations that do not match word for word. These accounts are complementary, not contradictory—they merely emphasize different points. Each author records what is important to himself as an historian. No one gives all the details of any account they record. Therefore, the details can vary.

In addition, it must be remembered that Jesus often spoke in Aramaic, while the writers of Scripture wrote their accounts in Greek. This means they had to translate those portions into Greek.

One gospel writer would use slightly different words from another writer to describe the same incident. However, all of the accounts gave the same meaning.

6. INERRANCY ALLOWS FOR VARIETIES OF WRITING STYLES

Inerrancy allows each biblical author to use his own unique style, grammar, and vocabulary. For example, Luke is written in very good Greek, while John's gospel is composed in rather elementary Greek. Paul writes with a lot of emotion, while Matthew gets straight to the point. Inerrancy allows for these differing styles.

7. INERRANCY ALLOWS QUOTATIONS FROM THE OLD TESTAMENT THAT ARE NOT WORD FOR WORD

Inerrancy allows for quotations from the Old Testament to be paraphrases rather than word-for-word translations. Actually, there is no other way this could have been done.

The New Testament writers had to translate the Old Testament when citing references since the New Testament was written in Greek while the Old Testament was written in Hebrew with small portions in Aramaic. Translation, therefore, was necessary.

8. INERRANCY ALLOWS FOR DEPARTURE FROM STANDARD FORMS OF GRAMMAR

The writers of Scripture have to be allowed to express the truth in whatever grammatical form they wish—not some standard or rule that someone else may insist upon. The doctrine of inerrancy allows for departure from standard forms of grammar.

Thus, we can say that God supernaturally kept the human author from any error but, in doing so, He did not dictate the exact form of their message—and this includes grammatical irregularities.

9. INERRANCY ALLOWS FOR PROBLEM PASSAGES TO EXIST

Inerrancy allows for problem passages that presently have no solution. This is to be expected with a work that was written by so many different authors, and spans so much time as the Bible. It is not reasonable to assume that all the problems will be easily solvable.

The solutions to problems presently found in the text await either the archaeologist's spade or further research into the biblical languages. There are some other cases where the solution may never be found.

While waiting for a solution to a Bible difficulty it is proper to take this biblical stance toward Scripture—there are no errors or contradictions in its pages. Belief in inerrancy leads Christians to approach the Scripture with an attitude of faith and trust as well as patience when faced with problem passages.

The reason people accept the inerrancy of Scripture is not because they have worked through all of its problems and have come up with reasonable solutions but rather because this is the view of Christ and His apostles toward the Scripture. This point should not be missed.

10. NOT EVERY STATEMENT CAN BE PROVEN TO BE INERRANT

Again, we must emphasize that the term inerrancy does not cover every statement that is contained in the Bible. There are a number of statements, by definition, that cannot be verified in the normal course of historical or scientific investigation. These statements that are outside the realm of being proven to be true or false are nevertheless totally trustworthy.

Therefore, when we say that the Bible is inerrant, we mean that it is totally trustworthy in everything that it records.

CONCLUSION: ANY DOCTRINE OF INERRANCY MUST HAVE THESE QUALIFICATIONS

Therefore, when we speak of the inerrancy or the trustworthiness of Scripture, we must keep these qualifications in mind. This doctrine must be properly understood to have an accurate view about what the Bible says about itself.

SUMMARY TO QUESTION 2
WHAT ARE SOME IMPORTANT CLARIFICATIONS TO THE DOCTRINE OF INERRANCY?

There are a number of important clarifications for a proper doctrine of the inerrancy of the Bible.

First, the doctrine of inerrancy means that the writers of Scripture conformed to the standards of accuracy for the day—not as modern historians would present the documents of the past.

In addition, inerrancy allows for non-technical descriptions of things. Inerrancy also allows the writers of Scripture to use pictorial language.

The doctrine of inerrancy does not always call for scientific precision. The writers of Scripture also may use different words to describe the same event. Inerrancy allows for a number of different writing styles in Scripture.

Inerrancy also permits the writers of the New Testament to cite the Old Testament without quoting it word for word.

The writers of Scripture are also permitted to express God's truth in whatever grammatical form they wished to employ. Inerrancy allows for problem passages to exist.

Finally, it is also important to emphasize that the term inerrancy does not cover all types of statements found in Scripture.

Does The Bible Testify
To Its Own Inerrancy?

Christians have often been accused of claiming something about the Bible that it does not claim for itself—that it is inerrant. Indeed, the term "inerrancy" is not found in Scripture. Neither is the doctrine of inerrancy directly taught.

It would be terrible if Christians claimed more for the Bible than what it claimed for itself. On the other hand, it would be equally tragic if Christians claimed less for the Bible than what the Scripture actually claimed for itself. What then, does the Scripture say about the subject?

INERRANCY SUMS UP WHAT THE BIBLE SAYS ABOUT GOD AND HIS WORD

A close examination of the evidence will show that the doctrine of inerrancy logically follows what the Bible says about God and itself.

This can be seen in the following ways.

First, God's character is absolutely perfect—there are no flaws in it.

Next, we find that God told certain of the biblical authors exactly what to say, and what to write. Since these words would have come direct from God, they would have been without any imperfection and error.

Third, the Scriptures directly testify that God's words are without error—He does not lie.

Fourth, all Scripture ultimately derives from the perfect, holy God who does not lie.

Finally, the Bible emphasizes that God's Word is the only standard of truth.

The biblical evidence for this is as follows.

1. GOD'S CHARACTER IS ONE OF ABSOLUTE PERFECTION

The idea that Scripture is without any error is consistent with the character of God. We find the Scripture emphasizing that God's character is one of absolute perfection—He is faithful and true.

Paul wrote to the Romans about God's faithfulness:

> Then what advantage has the Jew? Or what is the value of circumcision? Much in every way. To begin with, the Jews were entrusted with the oracles of God. What if some were unfaithful? Does their faithlessness nullify the faithfulness of God? By no means! Let God be true though every one were a liar, as it is written, That you may be justified in your words, and prevail when you are judged" (Romans 3:1-4 ESV).

The New Living Translation says it this way:

> Then what's the advantage of being a Jew? Is there any value in the Jewish ceremony of circumcision? Yes, being a Jew has many advantages. First of all, the Jews were entrusted with the whole revelation of God. True, some of them were unfaithful; but just because they broke their promises, does that mean God will break his promises? Of course not! Though everyone else in the world is a liar, God is true. As

the Scriptures say, "He will be proved right in what he says, and he will win his case in court" (Romans 3:1-4 NLT).

The Scriptures repeatedly affirm that God is a God of truth and light. John made the following statement that sums up the teaching of Scripture:

> Now this is the gospel message we have heard from him and announce to you: God is light, and in him there is no darkness at all (1 John 1:5 NET).

The united testimony of Scripture is that God is absolutely perfect—He has no imperfections. Of this, there is no doubt. John wrote:

> Then Jesus, still teaching in the temple courts, cried out, "Yes, you know me, and you know where I am from. I am not here on my own, but he who sent me is true. You do not know him" (John 7:28 NIV).

Elsewhere we find Jesus saying:

> I have many things to say and to judge about you, but the Father who sent me is truthful, and the things I have heard from him I speak to the world (John 8:26 NET).

God is a God of truth. In fact, the Holy Spirit is called the Spirit of truth. Jesus said:

> The Spirit of truth, whom the world cannot receive, because it neither sees Him nor knows Him; but you know Him, for He dwells with you and will be in you (John 14:17 NKJV)

This is another indication that everything that proceeds from God is the truth. Denial of this truth is a denial of the perfect character of God.

2. GOD GAVE THE BIBLICAL WRITERS THE WORDS THEY SHOULD SPEAK AND WRITE

The God of the Bible is perfect and holy. In Scripture, we are told that on many occasions this holy God gave certain people the exact words that they were to speak. An example of this is Moses:

> But Moses said to the LORD, "Please, Lord, I have never been a skilled speaker. Even now, after talking to you, I cannot speak well. I speak slowly and can't find the best words."
>
> Then the LORD said to him, "Who made a person's mouth? And who makes someone deaf or not able to speak? Or who gives a person sight or blindness? It is I, the LORD. Now go! I will help you speak, and I will teach you what to say" (Exodus 4:10-12 NCV).

If God gave Moses the exact words that he was to speak, it logically follows that these words would be without error.

We are later told that God commanded Moses to write down certain things. This is recorded in the Book of Exodus. It says:

> The LORD said to Moses: Write these words; in accordance with these words I have made a covenant with you and with Israel (Exodus 34:27 NRSV).

Since God told Moses what to write, the logical assumption is that these written words were also without error.

There is more. The authors of Scripture make it clear that they are recording the very Word of the Living God!

Consequently, the people were told not to add to or subtract from that which God commanded. Moses wrote:

> Now, Israel, listen to the statutes and the judgments which I am teaching you to perform, so that you will live and go in and

take possession of the land which the LORD, the God of your fathers, is giving you. You shall not add to the word which I am commanding you, nor take away from it, so that you may keep the commandments of the LORD your God which I am commanding you (Deuteronomy 4:1,2 NASB 2020).

Later, in the Book of Deuteronomy, the Lord describes how a true prophet of God should speak. We read the following:

But if a prophet says something I did not tell him to say as though he were speaking for me, or if a prophet speaks in the name of other gods, that prophet must be killed (Deuteronomy 18:20 NCV).

Obviously, God's Words were important to Him. The remainder of the Old Testament contains thousands of statements that claim to record the exact words of God. For example, the prophet Isaiah wrote:

Hear the word of the LORD, you rulers of Sodom; listen to the law of our God, you people of Gomorrah (Isaiah 1:10 NIV).

Over one hundred times in the Book of Jeremiah we find statements such as "the Word of the Lord came unto me." For example, it says:

The word of the LORD came to him in the thirteenth year of the reign of Josiah son of Amon king of Judah . . . The word of the LORD came to me, saying (Jeremiah 12,4 NIV).

On over sixty occasions, Ezekiel claimed that his words were God's words:

And he said to me, "Son of man, listen carefully and take to heart all the words I speak to you. Go now to your country-men in exile and speak to them. Say to them, ''This is what the Sovereign LORD says,' whether they listen or fail to lis-ten" (Ezekiel 3:10,11 NIV).

Daniel claimed to have heard the voice of God:

> Then I heard him speaking, and as I listened to him, I fell into a deep sleep, my face to the ground. A hand touched me and set me trembling on my hands and knees (Daniel 10:9 NIV)

Similar Claims Are Found In The New Testament

We find the same sort of claims in the New Testament. The gospels record that Jesus said that His teaching came from God:

> Jesus answered, "The things I teach are not my own, but they come from him who sent me" (John 7:16 NCV)

Jesus also said that God the Father gave Him the words to speak. He said to His disciples:

> I have not spoken on my own. Instead, the Father who sent me told me what I should say and how I should say it (John 12:49 God's Word).

Paul wrote to the Thessalonians that he was actually preaching the message of God:

> And we also thank God continually because, when you received the word of God, which you heard from us, you accepted it not as a human word but as it actually is, the word of God, which is indeed at work in you who believe (1 Thessalonians 2:13 NIV).

Therefore, it is the constant claim of the writers of Scripture that a great part of what they wrote consisted of direct words that God spoke to them. Because they were the words of God, these words were accepted without question or discussion.

Thus, to say Scripture is not inerrant and infallible is to speak against God. He has declared His Word to be true. The psalmist wrote:

All your words are true; all your just laws will stand forever (Psalm 119:60 NLT).

We should have the same attitude toward the Scripture as the psalmist expressed.

3. THE WORDS THAT COME FROM GOD ARE ALWAYS TRUE

We have seen that God is a God of truth and the Scripture records the exact words that God gave to the prophets.

There is more. We find that Scripture testifies that His Words are always reliable and true. Isaiah records the Lord saying:

> I have not spoken in secret, in some hidden place. I did not tell Jacob's descendants, 'Seek me in vain. I am the Lord, the one who speaks honestly, who makes reliable announcements' (Isaiah 45:19 NET).

The Lord speaks honestly and makes reliable announcements.

In Proverbs, we read the following about the words of God:

> Every word of God *is* pure; He *is* a shield to those who put their trust in Him. Do not add to His words, lest He rebuke you, and you be found a liar (Proverbs 30:5,6 NKJV).

His Word is pure; true in all that it states.

The Psalmist also stressed that God's words were reliable. He wrote:

> The Lord's words are absolutely reliable. They are as untainted as silver purified in a furnace on the ground, where it is thoroughly refined (Psalm 12:6 NET).

Peter emphasized that the Word of God was without any corruption whatsoever. He wrote the following to his readers:

You have been born anew, not of perishable but of imperishable seed, through the living and enduring word of God. For "All flesh is like grass and all its glory like the flower of grass. The grass withers, and the flower falls but the word of the Lord endures forever." That word is the good news that was announced to you (1 Peter 1:23-25 NRSV).

James said the Word of God is the "Word of truth." He stated it this way:

In fulfillment of his own purpose he gave us birth by the word of truth, so that we would become a kind of first fruits of his creatures (James 1:18 NRSV).

GOD CANNOT LIE

Furthermore, the Bible says that God cannot lie. This is emphasized in both testaments. In the Book of Numbers, it says the following:

God is not a man, that he should lie, nor a son of man, that he should change his mind. Does he speak and then not act? Does he promise and not fulfill? (Numbers 23:19 NIV).

We read the following in the Book of First Samuel:

And he who is the Glory of Israel will not lie, nor will he change his mind, for he is not human that he should change his mind! (1 Samuel 15:29 NLT).

Paul wrote to Titus about God always telling the truth:

Paul, a bond-servant of God and an apostle of Jesus Christ, for the faith of those chosen of God and the knowledge of the truth which is according to godliness, in the hope of eternal life, which God, who cannot lie, promised long ages ago (Titus 1:1,2 NASB 2020).

The writer to the Hebrews also emphasized this. He wrote:

> God also bound himself with an oath, so that those who received the promise could be perfectly sure that he would never change his mind. So God has given us both his promise and his oath. These two things are unchangeable because it is impossible for God to lie. Therefore, we who have fled to him for refuge can take new courage, for we can hold on to his promise with confidence (Hebrews 6:17,18 NLT).

When God speaks, He always speaks the truth!

There is something else. Jesus gave a harsh rebuke to those who only told the truth while they were under oath. The Lord said:

> Again, you have heard that it was said to our ancestors, You must not break your oath, but you must keep your oaths to the Lord. But I tell you, don't take an oath at all: either by heaven, because it is God's throne; or by the earth, because it is His footstool; or by Jerusalem, because it is the city of the great King. Neither should you swear by your head, because you cannot make a single hair white or black. But let your word 'yes' be 'yes,' and your 'no' be 'no.' Anything more than this is from the evil one (Matthew 5:33-37 CSB).

We are to tell the truth at all times, not simply when we are under oath. This is a further indication that God expects truth from all of His creation. In doing so, we imitate Him.

In addition, God's speech is unlike human speech because God is not like humans—He is absolutely perfect. The prophet Balaam said.

> God is not a man, that he should lie, nor a son of man, that he should change his mind. Does he speak and then not act? Does he promise and not fulfill? (Numbers 23:19 NIV)

He is not like us; He does not lie.

4. ALL SCRIPTURE ULTIMATELY COMES FROM GOD

From Scripture, we find that God is a God without any imperfections. We also discover that much of Scripture contains His exact words that the prophets were to speak or to write down.

In addition, we are told that these words that come from God are said to be always truthful and reliable.

We now find that *all* Scripture ultimately comes from God. Paul said that *all* Scripture was "breathed out" by God. He wrote to Timothy:

> All Scripture is breathed out by God and profitable for teaching, for reproof, for correction, and for training in righteousness, that the man of God may be competent, equipped for every good work (2 Timothy 3:16,17 ESV).

If all Scripture is breathed-out by God, then the Scripture, being the product of God, must also be true. There is no other conclusion that can be drawn.

If the Bible is ultimately the work of God the Holy Spirit, then how could it not tell the truth or record something that did not take place? The answer is simple, it could not.

There is something else. Paul says that all Scripture is profitable for teaching, reproof, correction and training. How can any of these things be true if the Bible contained errors?

In what sense would the Bible be profitable if it contained mistakes in various places? What makes matters worse is that no two people can agree where the errors are!

THE BOOK OF PSALMS RECORDS THAT GOD'S WORD IS ENTIRELY TRUE:

> The entirety of Your word is truth, and every one of Your righteous judgments endures forever (Psalm 119:160 NKJV).

The New Living Translation reads as follows:

> All your words are true; all your just laws will stand forever
> (Psalm 119:160 NLT).

It is clear that the Bible assumes that all of its words ultimately come from the God of truth.

5. THE BIBLE IS THE ULTIMATE STANDARD OF TRUTH

Finally, we discover that God's Word is not only true, it is the ultimate standard of truth. In the Old Testament we read:

> Now then, Lord GOD, You are God, and Your words are truth; and You have promised this good thing to Your servant (2 Samuel 7:28 NASB 2020).

Jesus said:

> Set them apart in the truth; your word is truth (John 17:17 NET).

His Words are more than merely true—they are *truth*. They are the standard by which everything else is judged.

INERRANCY FITS THE BIBLICAL DATA

Therefore, from a look at what the Bible says about God's nature, and His Word, we conclude that the Scripture must be without error.

Simply stated, we find that a large part of the Bible consists of the words that God told the writers to speak and also to write down. These words came direct from a holy God who has no imperfections. If they spoke and wrote down these words that God directly gave them, then these words must be without error.

Elsewhere we are directly told that God cannot lie—He always tells the truth. In addition, we are told that *all* Scripture has God as its ultimate source. Therefore, all the words of Scripture would have their origin in the God of truth. Finally, the Scripture says that God's Words are the ultimate standard of truth.

To put it another way, how could a perfect God divinely inspire a Bible that contained errors and incorrect information? The obvious answer is, "He cannot." Whatever God does, He does it in an absolutely perfect way.

Consequently, we can use terms and descriptions such as inerrant, infallible, completely accurate, absolutely truthful, and authoritative in every respect, to describe what we find in Scripture. God spoke, He did not stutter!

SUMMARY TO QUESTION 3
DOES THE BIBLE TESTIFY TO ITS OWN INERRANCY?

While the word "inerrant" is not found in the Bible, nor is the concept directly taught, we do find that Scripture does give testimony to its own inerrancy. There are a number of basic concepts in the Scripture that speak to this issue.

First, God is a holy God—there are no imperfections in His character.

Second, the Bible contains many direct statements that claim to record the actual words that God spoke.

Third, Scripture also testifies that God always tells the truth.

Fourth, we are also told that the entire Bible ultimately comes from God.

Finally, the Bible says that God's words are the ultimate standard of truth.

If the entire Scripture contains the communication of God to humanity, then it can be logically inferred that its contents will reflect the perfect nature of God.

The logical result of these truths is that God's Word is without error in everything that it says.

Therefore, it is proper to call the Bible inerrant, infallible, or a number of other terms that Christians use to describe its nature.

In What Sense
Is The Bible Perfect?

Christians often speak about God's Word being "perfect." In fact, the Scripture itself testifies to its perfection. We read the following in Psalms:

The law of the Lord is perfect and preserves one's life. The rules set down by the Lord are reliable and impart wisdom to the untrained (Psalm 19:7 NET).

What do we mean by this idea? In what sense is the Bible perfect? There are several points that should be made.

1. THERE IS ABSOLUTE AND RELATIVE PERFECTION

It must be stressed that the word perfect can be used in an absolute or a relative sense. When applied to Scripture it must be applied in a relative sense.

Often times we find the language of Scripture doing what other languages do—it speaks in approximation. The words are imprecise, but nevertheless they are true.

2. THERE IS NO SUCH THING AS SCIENTIFIC PRECISION IN SCRIPTURE

The Bible does not speak in scientific language nor does it speak with scientific precision.

For example, there are several occasions in Scripture where numbers are given as approximations. They include the following.

THE AGE OF JESUS AT THE BEGINNING OF HIS MINISTRY IS AN EXAMPLE OF IMPRECISION

We do not know Jesus' exact age when He began His public ministry. Luke says the following about Him:

> When He began His ministry, Jesus Himself was about thirty years old, being, as was commonly held, the son of Joseph, the son of Eli (Luke 3:23 NASB 2020).

The age of Jesus is not precisely given—He was about thirty years of age. He could have been older or younger.

THE BIBLE GIVES AN IMPRECISE TIME OF THE TRANSFIGURATION

When speaking of the transfiguration of Jesus, Luke records the event in this manner:

> Now about eight days after these sayings he took with him Peter and John and James and went up on the mountain to pray (Luke 9:28 ESV).

Luke says that it occurred about eight days later—nothing more specific is given. Therefore, it could have been seven or nine days later. There is no attempt to be exact.

PAUL AND THE IMPRECISE NUMBER OF DISCIPLES AT EPHESUS

Paul met a number of disciples in Ephesus and then preached Jesus to them. These men responded and were converted to Christ. We are then told the following about them:

> There were about twelve men in all (Acts 19:7 NASB 2020).

Approximately twelve disciples were there—there could have been more, there could have been less. The description is meant to be imprecise.

WE DO NOT KNOW HOW MANY PEOPLE PAUL BAPTIZED

There is another illustration of imprecision in the number of people that Paul baptized. He wrote the following to the church at Corinth:

> I thank God that I baptized none of you, but Crispus and Gaius; Lest any should say that I had baptized in mine own name. And I baptized also the household of Stephanas: besides, I know not whether I baptized any other (1 Corinthians 1:14-16 KJV).

Paul was not certain how many people he baptized. There is obviously no scientific precision in this example.

THERE ARE EXAMPLES IN SCRIPTURE OF NUMBERS ROUNDED OFF

We also find numerous examples in Scripture of numbers being rounded off.

For example, when Moses was told to take a census of the number of men available to fight, he wrote the following:

> Now the children of Reuben, Israel's oldest son, their gene-alogies by their families, by their fathers' house, according to the number of names, every male individually, from twenty years old and above, all who were able to go to war: those who were numbered of the tribe of Reuben were forty-six thousand five hundred. From the children of Simeon, their genealogies by their families, by their fathers' house, of those who were numbered, according to the number of names, every male individually, from twenty years old and above, all who were able to go to war: those who were numbered of

the tribe of Simeon were fifty-nine thousand three hundred
(Numbers 1:20-23 NKJV).

The numbers for each tribe were approximated in the same way (they
were rounded off to the nearest hundred).

Furthermore, the precise count of any nation or tribe would vary from
day to day with additions of births and subtractions by death. The
round numbers are specifically designed to be imprecise or approximate. The writers of Scripture, as well as its original readers, would
have understood this.

CONCLUSION: THE BIBLE MUST BE ALLOWED TO SPEAK IMPRECISELY AT TIMES

Therefore, when we speak of the Bible being perfect, it is relatively perfect not absolutely perfect. It is as perfect as it needs to be.

It is true in everything that it says, but sometimes the truths are only
approximate. Consequently, we should not expect to find precise scientific language, or scientific descriptions.

SUMMARY TO QUESTION 4
IN WHAT SENSE IS THE BIBLE PERFECT?

The Bible is perfect in the sense that it is true. What it records matches
with reality. However, we must be careful not to make the Bible try to
be something that it is not. It is not written in scientific language and
it is not scientifically exact.

We find that the Scripture speaks in approximations on a number of
occasions.

For example, Jesus was about thirty years of age when He began his
public ministry. It was about eight days after certain events when Jesus
was transfigured. There were about twelve disciples that Paul ministered

to in Ephesus. Neither does Paul specify exactly whom he baptized—he does not exactly recall how many there were.

In none of these examples do we find any precise numbers.

The lack of specificity can also be seen in the way the Bible handles large numbers. Many times, the large numbers are rounded off.

There is certainly nothing wrong, or errant, about writing in approximation. All languages do it.

Scripture is the communication of God's truth to humanity in the same forms that all of us understand. Consequently, speaking in approximation and rounding off numbers is something that we should expect from the Word of God.

What Is The Difference Between The Inerrancy Of Scripture And The Infallibility Of Scripture?

There are two theological terms that are often used to explain the nature of the Bible—inerrancy and infallibility. They are used to point out how the Bible is different from all other books that have ever been written. Many use these terms interchangeably. Infallibility means incapable of making a mistake while inerrancy means the absence of any error.

These concepts arose when the issue of the divine inspiration of the Bible was being addressed. Questions arose such as: In what sense, or to what degree, is the Bible the divinely inspired Word of God? How does it differ from all other books?

THE WORD INFALLIBLE MEANS TRUSTWORTHY

When referring to Scripture, the term infallible is usually used to mean reliable and trustworthy. It refers to something that is without any type of defect whatsoever. Those who trust its infallible teachings will never be led astray.

INERRANCY MEANS THERE ARE NO ERRORS WHATSOEVER

The term inerrancy is more recent. While some Christians use inerrancy and infallible interchangeably, they are normally used in slightly different ways.

Inerrancy contends that the Bible does not have any errors of fact or any statements that are contradictory. Inerrancy is more concerned with the details of Scripture.

INFALLIBILITY IS THE BROADER TERM

Infallibility deals more with the personal knowledge of the Lord rather than specific details. For example, one who believes in inerrancy will also believe in infallibility. The reverse, however, is not necessarily true.

There are those who argue that the Bible can contain errors of fact while still accomplishing its purpose—to bring humanity into a relationship with God. They see no problem trusting the Bible as the final standard of authority on all matters of faith and practice though it may contain some errors.

However, many others think that the idea of an infallible, but not an inerrant, Bible is something that is absolutely nonsensical.

THERE ARE THREE BASIC POSITIONS AMONG BIBLE BELIEVERS WITH RESPECT TO INERRANCY

With respect to the importance of the inerrancy issue, Bible believers usually take one of three positions. They include the following.

1. INERRANCY IS TRUE AND SHOULD BE USED AS A TEST OF FELLOWSHIP

This position holds that the doctrine of inerrancy is the only consistent Christian doctrine to hold concerning the nature of the Bible. Those who claim to believe in Jesus, yet reject the doctrine of inerrancy, should not be welcomed in Christian fellowship until they repent. Indeed, because inerrancy is such an important doctrine, it should be used as a test of fellowship. There is no room for compromise on such a vital issue.

2. INERRANCY, WHILE TRUE, SHOULD NOT BE USED AS A TEST OF FELLOWSHIP

This perspective believes the doctrine of inerrancy is true but does not make it a test of fellowship among believers. This view allows for believers to be inconsistent in their idea of the nature of the Scripture without assuming they should be avoided by other Christians.

3. INERRANCY MAY BE TRUE BUT SHOULD NOT BE USED AS A TEST OF FELLOWSHIP

The third position holds that inerrancy may or may not be true. However, it should not be made a test for fellowship with believers. It is irrelevant.

The inerrancy of Scripture was never made a test of Christian orthodoxy in the past because no one seemed to doubt it. Those who stress the doctrine of inerrancy stress the divine side of Scripture while also admitting the human side.

Those who do not necessarily embrace inerrancy stress the human side of Scripture.

These are the various positions that Christians hold.

SUMMARY TO QUESTION 5
WHAT IS THE DIFFERENCE BETWEEN THE INERRANCY OF SCRIPTURE AND THE INFALLIBILITY OF SCRIPTURE?

While the words "inerrancy" and "infallibility" are usually used interchangeably, there are some Bible students who make a distinction between the two.

Infallibility has the idea of being trustworthy while inerrancy goes further and says that the Scriptures contain no errors whatsoever.

Believers respond to the concept of inerrancy in a number of different ways. Some assume it should be used as a test of fellowship with other believers, while there are those who do not feel it is where the line should be drawn.

There are also those Christians who are not necessarily convinced by the doctrine of inerrancy—they think ones belief or non-belief in inerrancy is irrelevant.

Consequently, they do not see it as a burning issue.

QUESTION 6

What Are The Consequences When Doctrine Of Inerrancy Is Rejected?

Some argue that the doctrine of inerrancy is not that important. They believe the key issue is a person's relationship to Jesus Christ—not whether the Bible may or may not contain errors.

However, those who advocate an errant Scripture have seriously undermined the Bible's authority.

The following points need to be made about what occurs when the doctrine of inerrancy is denied.

1. THE BIBLE WOULD BE TESTIFYING FALSELY ABOUT ITSELF

A denial of inerrancy means that Scripture is incorrect when declaring God's words are never wrong. Consequently, when the Bible says that God's words are true, it is telling a lie.

If a person denies the doctrine of inerrancy, in effect, they are denying God's Word. The Lord tells us His Word is pure. In the Book of Proverbs, we read:

> Every word of God *is* pure; He *is* a shield to those who put their trust in Him. Do not add to His words, Lest He rebuke you, and you be found a liar (Proverbs 30:5,6 NIV).

If there are any mistakes in that Word, then it is not pure. The Bible says that His Word is truth. Jesus said:

> Set them apart in the truth; your word is truth (John 17:17 NET).

Yet, if it contains errors, then it is not truth. It has to be one or the other. The Word of God is either totally true or it is not. If it is not, then God has revealed Himself to humanity through untruths. Therefore, those who deny inerrancy are denying God's Word.

2. GOD WOULD BE A LIAR IF THERE ARE ERRORS IN SCRIPTURE

If there are errors in Scripture, then God simply has not told us the truth concerning it. This would make God a liar.

This brings up a simple question. Can we, therefore, trust anything that the Bible says?

Indeed, if God is capable of speaking falsely on some matters, then He is capable of speaking falsely on all matters. We would never know when we could trust Him.

Thus, those who accuse the Scripture of errors are also accusing the ultimate author of Scripture, God, of being a liar.

If God somehow spoke falsely, no matter how incidental the reference, this still constitutes an untruth. God cannot be both the God of truth and the God of untruth at the same time. The idea of God being untruthful in any matter is not found in Scripture.

3. ALL OF SCRIPTURE BECOMES OPEN TO SUSPICION IF THERE ARE ANY ERRORS

Even if the so-called errors are in "minor" matters, the Bible is now opened up to suspicion in all other areas—including the major doctrines of the faith. If inerrancy falls, then all other Bible doctrines will eventually fall also.

Without a clear Word from God, we are left without a firm foundation on *any* subject. Each individual would be the final determiner as to what God's truth is and what is not God's truth.

The Christian faith would be built upon sand, not upon the solid foundation of God's Word. Jesus, however, said His Word was built upon a rock:

> Therefore whoever hears these sayings of Mine, and does them, I will liken him to a wise man who built his house on the rock (Matthew 7:24 NKJV).

The words of Scripture are built either on the rock, or on the sand. An errant Bible makes the foundation one of sand.

Again, why should anyone trust anything that God says if we determine He has told us an untruth in one place in Scripture? This makes the entire Bible suspect.

If God is capable of speaking falsely once, then He is capable of doing it more than once. Logically, we could not really trust anything that He said. We would never read Scripture with confidence.

4. DENIAL OF INERRANCY GIVES CHRISTIANS THE RIGHT TO LIE

If one is convinced that God, on occasion, spoke untruthful things, does this mean that it should be allowable for believers to do the same thing?

The Bible commands believers to imitate God. Paul wrote:

> Therefore be imitators of God, as beloved children (Ephesians 5:1 NASB 2020).

Since we are commanded to imitate God does this allow believers to speak untruths in certain situations? Should we not imitate God and lie when we think it is necessary?

Those who reject an inerrant Bible give believers a basis for lying. If God intentionally spoke falsely, then why can't we do the same for the "greater good?"

5. BELIEVERS WILL LOOK TO OTHER SOURCES OF AUTHORITY FOR GUIDANCE

If someone does not believe the Bible is the divinely inspired and inerrant Word of God, then what is to stop them from turning to other sources as their ultimate authority? What they believe and practice will now be based upon church tradition, experience, unaided human reason, the changing views of modern unbelieving science, or mysticism. All of these avenues will lead them astray from the truth of God.

6. THE BEHAVIOR OF THE BELIEVER WILL CHANGE

The denial or even diluting of inerrancy will eventually result in lack of confidence in God's Word. It cannot be otherwise. This, in turn, may affect the way in which we behave.

If we do not believe everything that the Bible teaches, then why should we follow any of it? A Christian who rejects the inerrancy of Scripture may deviate only a little from following Christ, or they may deviate to a great degree.

Whatever the case may be, they will deviate. Consequently, the denial of inerrancy will eventually be spiritually destructive in the life of the believer.

7. THERE WILL BE A LOSS OF INTEREST IN STUDYING SCRIPTURE

Denial of inerrancy will cause the believer to lose interest in the studying of God's Word. If the Scripture contains errors, then why take the time to study it in detail? There is no need to attempt to find the meaning of the words of Scripture if these words are fallible.

Therefore, the idea of studying an errant Bible does not make sense.

8. THE ZEAL FOR MISSIONS AND EVANGELISM WILL BE LOST

One of the results of denying an inerrant Scripture is often the loss of zeal for preaching the gospel of Christ and reaching the lost. If the Bible is errant, then it may be errant concerning the situation of those who have not believed in Jesus.

Why then, should a person dedicate his or her life to reaching these people with the gospel?

9. NON-CHRISTIANS WILL HAVE NO REASON TO BELIEVE IN JESUS

Finally, there is the result of preaching and teaching an errant Bible for the non-believer. There is certainly no reason why non-Christians should embrace Christianity if the source of teaching, the Bible, is errant.

The Bible becomes like any other book written by humans. Why then should any non-Christian desire to become a Christian if the sacred book of the faith is one that contains errors?

These are some of the logical results for denying the biblical doctrine of inerrancy. While not everyone who denies the inerrancy of Scripture necessarily follows each of these steps, there is certainly no logical reason why they should not.

These points demonstrate why the doctrine of inerrancy is vitally important. Our attitude toward the Lord and Scripture should be that of the psalmist:

> The LORD exists forever; your word is firmly fixed in heaven (Psalm 119:89 NRSV).

The doctrine of inerrancy emphasizes that we do have a Word from God that is firmly fixed in the heavens.

SUMMARY TO QUESTION 6
WHAT ARE THE CONSEQUENCES WHEN THE DOCTRINE OF INERRANCY IS REJECTED?

The doctrine of inerrancy is important. Denial of inerrancy would be a denial of God's truthfulness to us. He would be a liar if the Bible contained error.

In addition, if one denies inerrancy, then the truth of the entire Bible comes under suspicion. Believers would be left without any solid foundation for faith. No one would be certain what was true and what was not.

In fact, lack of belief in inerrancy opens the door to denying the major doctrines of the Christian faith. One of the first doctrines to be rejected is salvation through Jesus Christ alone.

While this may not happen with each person who rejects an inerrant Scripture, it is the logical result of denying inerrancy.

Can The Scripture Be Trustworthy If It Makes Mistakes In Scientific And Historically Statements? (Limited Inerrancy)

Can a person still rely on the Bible as being trustworthy if it contains some errors in its statements of history and science? Does the doctrine of inerrancy extend to all matters scientific and historical?

Some people do not believe so. They teach that a person can accept the biblical teaching about God, heaven, hell, salvation, etc. without accepting the statements the Bible makes concerning historical or scientific matters.

This view is known variously as "revelational inerrancy," "dynamic inspiration," or "limited inerrancy."

There is also the view that the writers of Scripture were inerrant only that they faithfully reproduced the sources of their information. However, the sources themselves, may have been in error.

CLAIM: THE PURPOSE OF THE SCRIPTURES: TO MAKE US WISE UNTO SALVATION: IT IS NOT NECESSARILY INERRANT

Those who hold the view of limited inerrancy often emphasize that the purpose of Scripture is to make one "wise unto salvation," or give unbelievers, "wisdom unto salvation." Paul wrote to Timothy about the purpose of Scripture:

You, however, continue in the things you have learned and become convinced of, knowing from whom you have learned them (2 Timothy 3:14,15 NASB 2020).

Consequently, the incidental details of the events that are recorded in Scripture may or may not have happened. The important thing is that the message of salvation from sin comes across—not whether certain historical details actually occurred. Scripture is thus inerrant in purpose, but not inerrant in all its details.

In other words, through the Scripture, God accomplishes that which He desires even though there may be some factual errors.

THE VIEW THAT THERE ARE ERRORS IN THE SOURCES

There is also the point of view that the biblical writers were error-free in the sense that they faithfully copied, or reproduced, their sources. The sources of their information, both written and oral, were accurately recorded by the biblical writers.

However, this does not mean that the sources they used were without error. These sources could have been mistaken. Thus, the biblical writers faithfully reproduced error without correcting it.

What are we to make of these positions?

IS LIMITED INERRANCY AN OPTION?

According to many, it is proper to make the distinction between the theological and historical statements. Is this position of limited inerrancy an option for Christians?

We find that the Bible makes no such distinction between theological and historical statements. On the contrary, the Bible teaches that all Scripture is breathed out by God:

All Scripture is breathed out by God and profitable for teaching, for reproof, for correction, and for training in righteousness, that the man of God may be competent, equipped for every good work (2 Timothy 3:16,17 ESV).

This verse not only teaches that all Scripture is God-breathed, it also says that the purpose of Scripture is that believers might be mature and completely equipped for every good work.

How could the Scripture be profitable, and the believer equipped for every good work, if the Bible was full of errors? The Bible does not place any restriction on the subjects upon which it speaks truthfully about. All Scripture is profitable.

A number of points need to be emphasized.

1. SCRIPTURE ASSUMES THAT ALL EVENTS RECORDED ACTUALLY OCCURRED

The Scripture makes it clear that all the events it records literally occurred. Nowhere do we find any of the biblical writers casting the slightest doubt on any other part of Scripture.

To the contrary, they assumed that everything recorded was absolutely true in all its details. Of this, there is not the slightest doubt.

2. THERE IS NO BIBLICAL EVIDENCE OF A LIMITED INERRANCY

Scripture gives no evidence that its authority is limited in any way. There is no hint that any of the biblical statements, whether historical or theological, should be questioned. To make such a distinction is neither needful, nor helpful.

The inerrancy of Scripture does extend to all matters scientific and historic. Evidence is lacking in the statements of Scripture for the notion that the Word is a product of a division of labor—God working with the writers on doctrinal matters while leaving the biblical writers to their own fallible wisdom on historical and scientific matters. This is not what happened.

The New Testament writers trusted every detail of the Old Testament. For example, Paul stressed that he believed "everything" that was written in the Law and the Prophets:

> But I admit that I follow the Way, which they call a sect. I worship the God of our ancestors, and I firmly believe the Jewish law and everything written in the books of prophecy (Acts 24:14 NLT).

On the day of His resurrection, Jesus said that everything that was written in the Old Testament must be fulfilled:

> He said to them, "O how unwise and slow you are to believe in your hearts all that the prophets have spoken! Didn't the Messiah have to suffer these things and enter into His glory?" (Luke 24:25,26 CSB).

Notice that Jesus said *all* that the Old Testament prophets said should be believed; there were no exceptions.

3. THERE ARE OTHER IMPORTANT PURPOSES IN THE SCRIPTURE

Furthermore, the fact that the relationship between God and humanity is the main concern of Scripture does not comment one way or another about the Bible's truthfulness in areas of history and science. Other passages do this. These passages make it clear that all parts of Scripture are the true words of God.

The fact that the purpose of Scripture is to make its readers "wise unto salvation" certainly does not exclude it from being inerrant on other matters. It does not logically follow that if the Bible stresses one thing, it makes misstatements on things it emphasizes less.

In addition, while the main purpose of Scripture may be to bring the message of salvation to its readers, this does not mean that there are no other important purposes.

In short, the main concern of Scripture is not the only concern.

4. THERE WOULD BE NO BASIS OF AUTHORITY WITH A LIMITED INERRANCY

There is more. If the biblical writers were mistaken in their historical, geographical and scientific references then why, one might ask, should their statements in the theological realm be trusted?

It is meaningless to assert that the biblical writers made errors in history, science, and geography, but were kept error-free when they recorded statements in the theological realm (heaven, hell, salvation, etc.). We may rightly ask, "In what sense is the Bible divinely inspired?"

5. THE IDEA OF REPRODUCING ERRANT SOURCES MAKES THE DOCTRINE OF INERRANCY MEANINGLESS

Finally, the idea that some hold that the biblical writers faithfully reproduced sources that had errors in it makes the end result of Scripture in doubt.

While this perspective is held by some Christians, it is does not instill much confidence in the Bible. Many parts of the Bible consist of the writer using sources. This includes the early chapters of Genesis and the entire gospel of Luke.

According to this view, the creation account recorded in Genesis, as well as Luke's entire gospel, is now suspect.

Moses, the writer of Genesis, had to compile his work from sources. Though he may have had written sources from the time of Adam and Eve, he certainly did not have any written sources before human beings were created!

At the very least, the creation account in the first chapter of Genesis now becomes suspect. Furthermore, the remainder of the Book of Genesis, which is based upon some type of source, either oral or written, likewise becomes suspect.

In his prologue, Luke explained that his entire gospel was based upon sources. Therefore, his entire work now comes under suspicion. While some may argue that both Moses and Luke faithfully reproduced the information from their sources, it is no benefit for us whatsoever if these sources contained errors.

CONCLUSION: THE SCRIPTURE MUST ALWAYS BE CORRECT

The Bible must be correct on things that can be verified. While it is not a textbook on history, the historical references must be accurate. While the Bible is not a textbook on science, its statements of a scientific nature must be accurate. If the Bible cannot be trusted in areas in which it can be verified, then why should we trust it in areas, which by definition, cannot be verified? Jesus said:

> If I have told you about earthly things and you do not believe, how can you believe if I tell you about heavenly things? (John 3:12 NRSV).

We must believe the earthly as well as the heavenly things that God has told us. All of God's words are important. This is why the Bible commands not to add or subtract from them. The Bible says:

> Don't add to these commands, and don't leave anything out, but obey the commands of the LORD your God that I give you. (Deuteronomy 4:2 CEV).

The Bible says there are severe penalties for adding or subtracting to what God has revealed:

> I testify to everyone who hears the words of the prophecy of this book: if anyone adds to them, God will add to him

the plagues that are written in this book; and if anyone takes away from the words of the book of this prophecy, God will take away his part from the tree of life and from the holy city, which are written in this book. (Revelation 22:18-19 NASB 2020).

Paul wrote to the Romans about the necessity to believe everything that was written:

For whatever was written before was written for our instruction, so that through our endurance and through the encouragement of the Scriptures we may have hope (Romans 15:4 CSB).

It is important that we believe that everything in Scripture has been put there for a purpose, even the so-called incidental details.

Another problem with this point of view is to determine exactly which statements are divinely inspired, and which are not. The questions that immediately arise are these: Who decides what is true? How can one differentiate between facts and teaching? How can one separate the essential message of the teaching of the Bible from the background in which it is presented?

There is certainly no such distinction recognized in Scripture itself. Whoever does this sort of thing sets himself, or herself, above the Bible, and reverses roles with God.

Therefore, the doctrine of limited inerrancy causes more problems than it solves.

SUMMARY TO QUESTION 7
CAN THE SCRIPTURE BE TRUSTWORTHY IF IT MAKES MISTAKES IN SCIENTIFIC AND HISTORICALLY STATEMENTS? (LIMITED INERRANCY)

The doctrine of limited inerrancy believes that inerrancy does not extend to matters historical and scientific—only theological statements are error-free. The purpose of the Bible is to make its readers "wise unto salvation" —not to be an historically accurate record in every detail it presents.

Therefore, it is argued that the Bible can be considered totally trustworthy even if it makes some minor mistakes in matters of history, geography, and science.

This position cannot be justified biblically. Scripture treats all its events as literally occurring. In addition, there is no hint that the insignificant details recorded did not actually take place. All Scripture is assumed to be correct in everything that it says.

Furthermore, the main concern of Scripture, to bring salvation to its readers, is not the only concern of Scripture. The Bible testifies that it also reveals the true words of God to humanity in every place that it records God speaking. This includes the direct words of God, the words of the prophets, or the historical details recorded in Scripture.

The position of limited inerrancy also causes more problems than it solves. There must be some standard to determine what passages are theological and which are merely historical or scientific. Who will determine the standard?

Some may argue that the Bible can survive even if a small number of errors are found in it.

However, this may be the start of a downhill slide that will logically end in unbelief. Every part of the Bible will become suspect. Limited inerrancy is not a sufficient answer to the question of inerrancy.

In addition, those who argue that the biblical writers were inerrant only so far as to correctly reproduce their errant sources, likewise, give us a meaningless doctrine of inerrancy.

Therefore, a better answer must be found.

Why Do Some Christians Believe The Bible Contains Errors?

The fact is that there are a number of Christians who believe the Bible is God's divinely inspired Word to the human race, yet also believe it contains some errors or may contain errors.

Most believers who hold this view would say the errors are few in number and have nothing to do with the overall message.

What causes Christians to believe this? Why do they accept a Bible that may be imperfect? There are a number of possible reasons.

1. THEY ARE CONVINCED THAT THERE ARE GENUINE ERRORS IN SCRIPTURE

For a number of Christians, they hold to an errant Bible because they are convinced that there are genuine errors in Scripture. They see certain problems as unresolvable. Consequently, they assume the only honest thing to do is admit there is an error instead of trying to harmonize something that really cannot be harmonized.

This position is especially true for those who have done some type of advanced study in secular institutions. Technical problems regarding the Scripture are brought up and no solution is given. The assumption, or in many cases the outright claim, is that the problem is not resolvable. Therefore, errors must be admitted.

2. THEY DO NOT BELIEVE INERRANCY IS A BIBLICAL CONCEPT

Some people reject the idea of inerrancy because they do not believe inerrancy is a biblical concept. There is no passage that clearly teaches inerrancy, neither is the word "inerrancy" used in the Bible.

Accordingly, the inerrancy issue is a non-issue. They do not think it really matters, one way or another, whether the Bible is totally inerrant. Any errors in Scripture would be only in the incidental details that really have nothing to do with the main message.

Thus, we should not spend time in all the minute details of Scripture but rather proclaim the message of Christ and His forgiveness of sin. Since there seem to be errors in Scripture, the concept, as well as the term, should be abandoned.

3. INERRANCY IS A PURELY NEGATIVE CONCEPT

There is also the rejection of inerrancy because it is a negative concept— the Bible does not contain errors. Instead, we should be emphasizing the positive message of Scripture. The real message of the Bible is true even if there are a few small errors here and there.

Hence, they want to be positive about the nature of Scripture so they emphasize the Bible is God's truth to humanity even though there may be a few errors in it.

4. THEY DO NOT BELIEVE DENIAL OF INERRANCY LEADS TO UNBELIEF

Others do not see the logic of their position. They have accepted the fact that the Bible contains certain errors but the idea does not bother them. They have not really thought through what this may mean or they are not convinced that it will lead to unbelief.

While not everyone who accepts a Bible with errors will ultimately deny its truth, there is certainly nothing stopping people from doing such a thing.

5. CERTAIN PEOPLE MAY WANT TO APPEAR SCHOLARLY OR INTELLIGENT

There is also the likelihood that some people who deny inerrancy do so to appear wise in the eyes of others. This is especially true for those who work in academia. They want their colleagues to accept them as informed and intelligent. They do not want to appear to be ignorant.

Thus, they accept the prevailing idea among non-believing scholars with respect to the inerrancy of Scripture.

6. SOME MAY WANT TO HAVE AN EXCUSE FOR NOT OBEYING GOD'S WORD

The final reason why certain believers reject the idea of inerrancy has nothing to do with actual problems in Scripture—a belief that the Bible does not teach inerrancy, or some intellectual crisis they are having.

Some people use the idea of an errant Bible to disobey certain of the commands found in Scripture. While this is not necessarily true of every Christian who rejects the idea of biblical inerrancy, it is true of some.

By accepting the idea that the Bible has errors, this gives a person the excuse to obey, or disobey, portions of Scripture as they so choose. The reason for the rejection of inerrancy is not so much an intellectual crisis as it is a moral crisis.

RESPONSE

Whatever the reason, there are a number of Bible-believing Christians who do not accept the idea that the entire Bible is free from error.

However, the idea that God's Word somehow contains errors is not consistent with the totality of the teaching of Scripture on the subject. In fact, it is totally contradictory to it. A number of points need to be stressed.

First, while there are difficulties in Scripture, these difficulties are not the same as proven errors. Indeed, most difficulties have plausible solutions.

Those difficulties that do not presently have an obvious solution should not be assumed to be errors. This is because of the nature of the Bible. It is God's Book—His God-breathed Word—and He does not lie. As the God of truth, He would not mix truth with error in His Word.

If so, humans would be in the hopeless position of determining which was which. An error-filled revelation from God is as bad as no revelation at all. No consensus would ever be arrived at to determine which parts should be believed and which parts rejected.

Thus, those who reject the idea of inerrancy, either because the Bible does not use the word, or does not specifically teach the doctrine, are not being genuine will all the data. There really is no other conclusion to come to when the entire teaching of Scripture is considered.

While the salvation of the lost through Jesus Christ is the main message of Scripture, it certainly does not follow that there are no other important truths in Scripture.

One of these truths is that the living God has accurately, truly, and inerrantly revealed His truth to humankind through a number of sacred writings that now make up one Book—the Bible.

There is something else. While those who do not think that denial of inerrancy necessarily leads one to unbelief, they are not really thinking through the logic of this position.

Non-Christians would have no real basis to accept the truths of Scripture if it was proclaimed to them as a Book that has God's truth mixed with some error. They could conclude that this does not make the Bible different from any other so-called sacred Book that claims divine truth.

Indeed, Islam says that every word of *their* holy book, the Quran, was dictated by Allah to the prophet Muhammad. All of the Quran is true.

Yet, the Christian would be saying that this is not necessarily the case with their holy Book, the Bible. Such a position would not give the non-believer much motivation of investigating the claims of Scripture or believing it. Why should they?

The position of arguing for a Bible that has errors puts the authority of Scripture into the hands of fallible humans and not an infallible God.

We now become the judges of what is, and what is not, God's Word. Not only are we incapable of doing such a thing, it is also a blasphemous idea to think that we should even attempt this.

Thus, we conclude the doctrine of the inerrancy of Scripture is a vital one for a Christian to hold. Otherwise, there is no firm basis in which to live their own life or to tell others the message of Jesus.

SUMMARY TO QUESTION 8
WHY DO SOME CHRISTIANS BELIEVE THE BIBLE CONTAINS ERRORS?

There are a number of Christians who accept the Bible as God's holy Word yet deny that it is inerrant. The reasons as to why this happens can be summed up as follows.

First, some Christians believe there are actual errors in Scripture. Consequently, in an attempt to be intellectually honest, they admit this to be the case. Others do not believe the concept of inerrancy is clearly taught in the Bible. Thus, the entire idea is a non-issue. Therefore, they can accept the idea of a few errors in Scripture.

There is also the position that inerrancy is a negative concept that should be abandoned. The message of Scripture is Jesus Christ and His forgiveness of sin. It should be proclaimed in a positive way without insisting the Bible is error-free.

Others who think there are errors in the Bible do not feel this takes away from it being the Word of God. They do not believe it will eventually lead people to reject the entire message of Scripture because a few errors exist.

In the academic world, there are some believers who reject inerrancy for reasons other than intellectual. They do not want to appear less knowledgeable or less educated than those whom they work with. Consequently, they go along with the majority of non-Christian scholars who reject inerrancy.

Finally, there are personal reasons as to why some Christians would claim errors in Scripture. This is done because of a certain sin, or sins, in their life. In other words, they reject certain portions of the Bible that may be interfering with their current lifestyle.

In sum, it has absolutely nothing to do with intellectual problems with the Bible. By denying inerrancy, one may assume they can escape their responsibility to be obedient to the totality of Scripture.

However, this is certainly not the case!

What Is The Difference Between A Difficulty And A Contradiction?

The Bible claims to be the authoritative, inerrant Word of God and there is sufficient evidence to believe the claims of Scripture are true.

Yet when we read the Bible there are difficulties that we encounter. How are we to deal with these obvious difficulties? The following points need to be stressed.

THERE IS A DIFFERENCE BETWEEN A BIBLE DIFFICULTY AND AN OUTRIGHT CONTRADICTION

At first glance, there do seem to be contradictions that we encounter when we read the pages of Scripture. These difficulties, and so-called "contradictions" we find, are between different authors, and even within the writings of the same author. What are we to make of them?

We should note that there is a **difference** between a difficulty and a contradiction. A difficulty is something that, initially, is hard to make sense out of.

However, it is not necessarily a contradiction or error. It is merely something that causes a problem when we first look at it.

Unfortunately, too many people assume a difficulty is the same thing as an error. The Bible contains passages that are difficult to understand but when all the evidence is in, it cannot contradict itself. This is because there is only one ultimate author behind the text—God Himself.

THE ADMISSION OF SCRIPTURE CONCERNING DIFFICULTIES

Even the Bible itself admits that there are some difficult areas. Peter wrote the following concerning the writings of the Apostle Paul:

> Therefore, beloved, while you are waiting for these things, strive to be found by him at peace, without spot or blemish; and regard the patience of our Lord as salvation. So also our beloved brother Paul wrote to you according to the wisdom given him, speaking of this as he does in all his letters. There are some things in them hard to understand, which the ignorant and unstable twist to their own destruction, as they do the other scriptures (2 Peter 3:14-16 NRSV).

Peter admits that Paul wrote some things that were hard to understand.

WE ALL NEED HELP IN UNDERSTANDING THE SCRIPTURE

The Book of Acts gives us an example of Philip the evangelist having to explain the meaning of a difficult passage to the Ethiopian eunuch. It says:

> So Philip ran up to it and heard the man reading Isaiah the prophet. He asked him, "Do you understand what you're reading?" The man replied, "How in the world can I, unless someone guides me?" So he invited Philip to come up and sit with him (Acts 8:30,31 NET).

Like the Ethiopian eunuch, we all need help in understanding the things written in the Bible because there are matters that are difficult to understand.

THE DIFFICULTY MAY BE CLEARED UP LATER

Because a certain passage in Scripture is not completely understood right now, does not mean that it will never be understood. As our knowledge of the ancient world increases, the number of difficulties and obscurities continues to vanish. There are many examples of Bible difficulties having been cleared up due to recent knowledge. We must state categorically that there has never been one demonstrable error proven from the original text of Scripture!

THERE IS ONLY A SMALL MINORITY OF DIFFICULTIES IN SCRIPTURE

We must also emphasize that the message of the Bible is crystal clear and for the most part, the text of the Bible is likewise clear. Difficult passages constitute a *small* minority in the text. We are not dealing with difficulty after difficulty on every page.

CONCLUSION: THE CENTRAL MESSAGE OF THE BIBLE IS CLEAR

The most important point, that cannot be overemphasized, is that the central message of the Bible—Jesus Christ is humanity's only Savior— is not only clear, it is backed up by sufficient evidence to make any honest inquirer believe.

There are a few remaining difficulties that still need to be cleared up; however, this should not deter one from believing in Jesus Christ. Our knowledge will always be imperfect and thus faith must always be exercised. However, biblical faith is intelligent, not blind faith.

Mark Twain's famous statement is appropriate here. He said the statements that bothered him in the Bible were not the ones he did not understand, what bothered him were the things he did understand!

Another person has said it this way:

Many things in the Bible I cannot understand; many things in the Bible I only think I understand; but there are many things in the Bible I cannot misunderstand.

We must act upon those statements we cannot misunderstand.

SUMMARY TO QUESTION 9
WHAT IS THE DIFFERENCE BETWEEN A DIFFICULTY AND A CONTRADICTION?

There are difficulties in the Bible. A difficulty, however, is not the same as a contradiction. Because we do not have the answer to a certain Bible difficulty today does not mean that we will never find the answer. The more knowledge we have about the Bible and its past, the fewer difficulties we find in Scripture.

Since the Bible is God's inerrant Word, ultimately all difficulties will be able to be cleared up. However, even with the present difficulties found in Scripture, the message of the Bible is clear.

Why Should The Subject Of Bible Difficulties Be Discussed?

That there are difficulties in the Bible is a fact. How then, should the reader, in general, deal with the subject of Bible difficulties? What should we do when confronted with a difficult verse or passage?

There are a number of observations we can make.

BELIEVERS ARE NOT AFRAID OF DISCOVERING THE TRUTH

First, we should not be afraid to discuss so-called "contradictory" passages. There is nothing gained in overlooking the difficulties that are in Scripture. We should not have the attitude to just take everything by "blind faith."

The Bible encourages us to respond to questions. Paul wrote the following to the church at Colosse:

> Be wise in the way you act with people who are not believers, making the most of every opportunity. When you talk, you should always be kind and pleasant so you will be able to answer everyone in the way you should (Colossians 4:5,6 NCV).

Jesus said that the truth would set people free. John wrote:

> So Jesus said to the Jews who believed in him, "If you con-
> tinue to obey my teaching, you are truly my followers. Then
> you will know the truth, and the truth will make you free"
> (John 8:31,32 NCV).

Paul encouraged the king to "check out the facts" when it came to the
story of Jesus Christ. He said the following:

> For the king knows about these things, and to him I speak
> boldly. For I am persuaded that none of these things has
> escaped his notice, for this has not been done in a corner
> (Acts 26:26 ESV).

Truth is not something that the believer in Jesus Christ fears. To the
contrary, the believer welcomes the truth.

WE DO NOT KNOW EVERYTHING

In addition, we should not be afraid to ask tough questions about the
Christian faith. Seemingly, the older we get the more difficult it is for
us to admit we do not know certain things—it is tough to have to ask
questions. Some wrongly assume that asking questions shows signs of
weakness.

However, it is a mark of maturity to admit there are still many things in
this world that we do not know. Because we do not presently have an
answer, does not mean that we never will get the answer. If we do not
continue to ask, we will not continue to learn.

IT IS NOT LACK OF FAITH TO ASK QUESTIONS

For believers, we are not offending God by asking legitimate questions
about the Christian faith. Asking questions is not the same as unbelief. Asking honest questions will get us honest answers. Discussing the
questions with others is also a good idea. The Bible says:

Iron sharpens iron, and one man sharpens another (Proverbs 27:17 ESV).

The New Century Version says:

As iron sharpens iron, so people can improve each other (Proverbs 27:17 NCV).

The New Living Translation translates the verse as follows:

As iron sharpens iron, a friend sharpens a friend (Proverbs 27:17 NLT).

The idea is that honest questions should be faced, and that others can help with the answers.

ALL OF US NEED TO THINK

Unfortunately, some people do not like to think. It is more comfortable for them to merely hold on to preconceived notions and prejudices. When we come across difficult passages in Scripture, or sayings that we cannot quite understand, it is easier to fall back on what we have always believed rather than re-evaluate what the text might be saying.

This, however, is not the way we can grow in our Christian experience. We need to be able to assess what we believe in light of all the facts. If new information comes to us which causes us to change something we have previously believed, then we must be intellectually honest enough to admit that we have been wrong in the past.

WE SHOULD BE UNLIKE THE CULTS WHO BLINDLY OBEY THEIR LEADERS

Furthermore, we do not want to be like cultic groups that do not tolerate questions from their people. Honest answers from cult leaders would cause the leaders to lose control.

Christians should not blindly follow what some leader says—no matter who it is. Faith will only increase when our questions are answered. Blindly obeying favorite Bible teachers is not a scriptural attitude.

SOME OBSERVATIONS ON BIBLE DIFFICULTIES

There are a number of important observations that need to be made about the Bible difficulties that are in Scripture.

1. WE ARE NOT ALONE IN OUR PARTICULAR QUESTION

Chances are the questions that we have are not unique to us. Others have had the same problem as they have read Scripture and thought about the truth of the Christian faith.

It is highly doubtful that someone will come up with a new question about Christianity, or the Bible, that no one else has thought of in the history of the church.

2. THE DIFFICULTIES HAVE BEEN ANSWERED TIME AND AGAIN

The crucial questions regarding what God has done in history, as well as attempting to understand difficult biblical passages, are not unique to our generation. They have been answered time and time again.

Indeed, each question we have about the Bible has been asked and answered hundreds, if not thousands, of times since the time of Christ. The key is to discover where these answers can be found.

3. WE SHOULD ACCEPT THE ANSWER AND THEN GO ON

Once we receive an answer to our question, then we should go on. It is wrong to keep asking a question once the answer has been given.

Furthermore, it is also wrong to doubt the Bible when there are a number of possible answers to a particular question, yet we are not certain what the right answer is.

An example of this would be the problem of the two accounts of the genealogy of Jesus found in Matthew and Luke. There are, at least, four different ways of reconciling the two genealogies, yet we are not absolutely certain which the correct resolution is.

This does not mean these accounts are in error—it means we are not certain which of the possible answers is correct.

4. DIFFICULTIES ARE USED AS AN EXCUSE FOR NOT BELIEVING

Sometimes people use the difficulties in Scripture as an excuse for not believing in Jesus. They believe this will remove them of any responsibility.

Consequently, they use Bible difficulties as an excuse for not believing in Christ. They are blind to the evidence because they are willingly blind. Ultimately, they do not want to find a way to reconcile difficulties in Scripture.

Since they do not want to know the truth, any explanation that attempts to clear up a difficulty will fall upon deaf ears.

However, this does not remove the responsibility from them—as they would like to believe that it does. Scripture teaches that God will ultimately hold all of us responsible on how we deal with the evidence that He has presented to us.

The fact of difficulties in Scripture can sometimes remove those who are not genuinely interested in the truth of God's Word.

Indeed, God is on record as saying that He will condemn those who reject His clearly revealed Word. Paul wrote:

> But God shows his anger from heaven against all sinful, wicked people who push the truth away from themselves. For the truth about God is known to them instinctively. God

has put this knowledge in their hearts. From the time the world was created, people have seen the earth and sky and all that God made. They can clearly see his invisible qualities— his eternal power and divine nature. So they have no excuse whatsoever for not knowing God (Romans 1:18-20 NLT).

Unbelievers, though not interested in the truth of God, have no real excuse. Their ignorance is not excusable.

CONCLUSION: DIFFICULTIES SHOULD NOT KEEP US FROM BELIEVING THE MESSAGE OF SCRIPTURE

The fact that there are difficulties in the Bible should not keep anyone from believing the clear message of Scripture. We should not refuse to accept God's message because of a few difficulties found in the text.

If we remain ignorant of the things of God, it is only because we have self-imposed this darkness upon ourselves. The answers are there, but we must spend the time to find them. This can only come about from a serious study of the Word of God. This is what is needed when difficult passages of Scripture come our way.

SUMMARY TO QUESTION 10
WHY SHOULD THE SUBJECT OF BIBLE DIFFICULTIES BE DISCUSSED?

The subject of Bible difficulties should definitely be a topic of discussion. The biblical attitude toward difficult questions is to face them head-on. They should not be ignored or glossed over. It is not lack of faith to bring up the difficult areas in Scripture or to try to find an answer.

Once an answer to a particular difficulty is found, then we should move on. When these difficulties are cleared up after serious study, the reader is greatly benefited by the exercise.

QUESTION 11

What Are The Various Ways In Which Believers Approach Difficulties In Scripture?

All Bible believers admit that there are difficulties in Scripture. No one doubts this. However, not all Christians agree on how these difficulties should be approached.

Generally speaking, there are five basic approaches to the subject. We can summarize these various positions as follows.

OPTION 1: THERE SHOULD BE AN ATTEMPT TO HARMONIZE ALL DIFFICULTIES IN SCRIPTURE BECAUSE THERE ARE NO ERRORS

There is the position that all difficulties have an answer, and it is the responsibility of the believer to try to discover that answer and harmonize the difficulty.

In other words, it is the duty of believers to demonstrate that the Scriptures are what they claim to be—the error-free Word of God. Thus, each difficulty should be faced and answered.

OPTION 2: INERRANCY SHOULD BE ASSUMED BUT IT IS NOT NECESSARY TO TRY TO HARMONIZE DIFFICULTIES

Others who believe in the inerrancy of the Bible do not feel it is necessary for the believer to attempt to harmonize difficulties. There is so much evidence from the testimony of Scripture, as to its divine authority and inerrancy, that it is needless to spend time and energy harmonizing difficulties.

According to this position, the message of Scripture should be proclaimed, and the Bible should be preached and taught as being God's inerrant Word. This is where the Bible-believer should place his or her efforts.

OPTION 3: PROCLAIM THE WORD AND ANSWER DIFFICULTIES

This option is a balance between options one and two. The first duty of believers is to proclaim God's Word but when difficulties arise, then they should be dealt with; not merely ignored.

OPTION 4: ERRORS EXIST IN SCRIPTURE AND SHOULD BE ADMITTED

There are some Christians who believe the difficulties in Scripture cannot be harmonized because they are actual errors. They do not believe there is any way these difficulties can be honestly harmonized.

Consequently, they see errors as part of the Bible but do not think it really makes any difference.

OPTION 5: THERE ARE ERRORS IN SCRIPTURE BUT WITH THE SOURCES NOT THE WRITERS

A small minority of believers claim that some of the difficulties in Scripture are not the result of an error on the part of the biblical author, but rather upon the source the author used.

Such things as the genealogies, which were matters of public record, were infallibly reproduced by the writers of Scripture. However, these sources were not error free. So, what we have is an infallible reproduction of a source that contained errors.

WHAT IS THE BEST ANSWER?

These are the various ways in which believers have faced Bible difficulties. What, therefore, is the best answer?

The best answer seems to be the third option. The Bible is indeed without error and Christians should spend their time proclaiming the truth of the message.

However, difficulties should be faced, not ignored, and when necessary, harmonization of these difficulties should be done. There is no reason whatsoever to hold the fourth or fifth option that assumes the Bible contains errors. God's Word is without any type of error or contradiction.

SUMMARY TO QUESTION 11
WHAT ARE THE VARIOUS WAYS IN WHICH BELIEVERS APPROACH DIFFICULTIES IN SCRIPTURE?

The fact that the Bible contains difficulties has led Christians to respond to them in various ways. Some feel it is the duty of the believer to try to harmonize all difficulties. Others do not believe this is necessary. Scripture clearly teaches inerrancy and consequently the believer should not be that concerned with certain difficulties that seem to be errors.

Another view sees the truth as being a combination of options one and two. The duty of the believer is first and foremost to proclaim the message of Jesus Christ and assume that the Bible is without errors when doing so.

However, when difficulties arise, they should be faced and answered, not ignored. This seems to be the best answer to the problem.

Some feel there are errors in Scripture, and these errors should be admitted, but that the errors do not really matter.

Finally, a small minority of Christians contend the errors are in the sources the writers used, not with the writers themselves. Thus, the writers infallibly reproduced the errors found in their sources.

The fourth and fifth options are not necessary for believers to embrace. God's Word does not make mistakes.

What Type Of Difficulties Do We Find In Scripture?

There are a number of areas of difficulty that we face as we attempt to understand and interpret the Scripture. This is not surprising seeing that the books of Scripture were written between two and four thousand years ago in a different culture, and in three different languages—Hebrew, Aramaic, and Greek.

Consequently, we encounter a number of areas that are difficult for us to understand in our day and age. Some of these difficulties include the following.

1. THERE IS THE PROBLEM OF TIME BETWEEN THE BIBLICAL EVENTS AND TODAY

One of the basic reasons we find difficulties in Scripture is simply the problem of time. The various books of the Bible were written from two to four thousand years ago in an era that has long passed into history. Consequently, there is a time gap that needs to be bridged.

2. THE MEANING OF WORDS AND PHRASES IS PROBLEMATIC

The problem of language also comes into play when we read the Scripture. Most of us who read the Bible are not native Hebrew or

Greek speakers, neither are most of us Jewish. Even those who speak modern Greek or modern Hebrew are still separated by two to four thousand years of history in which the meaning of words and phrases change.

Since we are not first-century readers of the original languages, problems can and do occur when we attempt to understand the meaning of some words and phrases. Many of our problems result in our lack of understanding of the idiom of the day.

Incomplete knowledge of words and expressions can cause us difficulty in interpreting Scripture. This is especially true in the Old Testament where some of the words used are found only once in Scripture and nowhere else in the Hebrew language. This can create doubt as to their exact meaning.

3. THERE ARE TRANSLATIONAL MISUNDERSTANDINGS

Some of the difficulties we encounter are not really there—they are based upon a wrong understanding of the translation of a text. It is also possible that a particular translation a person is using has an unfortunate translation of a particular text.

This is why every reader should have, if possible, at least three Bible translations to consult. At times, simply reading a different translation of Scripture will clear up a difficulty.

4. WE FIND GRAMMATICAL DIFFICULTIES IN THE BIBLE

There are also some difficulties that are due to the grammatical construction in the original language. The more technical commentaries can help explain these grammatical difficulties.

5. THERE ARE CULTURAL DIFFICULTIES IN SCRIPTURE

The lack of understanding of the historical situation is another source of difficulty. Since biblical events took place in a different cultural setting than for those living in the Western world, those of us in the West need to understand some things about the cultural background to help us with the interpretation.

6. THERE ARE CERTAIN TEXTUAL DIFFICULTIES IN SCRIPTURE

Some of the difficulties in Scripture are due to questions about how the text should read. But this is mainly true in the Old Testament. The New Testament text is very secure.

7. SCRIPTURE RECORDS CHANGING CIRCUMSTANCES

The difficulties are sometimes due to the changing circumstances found in the different passages. For example, the Bible says that everything was originally created good.

The Book of Genesis reads:

> Then God looked over all he had made, and he saw that it was excellent in every way. This all happened on the sixth day (Genesis 1:31 NLT).

Yet after humanity sinned against God (Genesis 3) things were no longer good. What was true before the Fall of humanity was not necessarily true after the Fall because of the changed circumstances.

Therefore, when we read the Bible, we must appreciate that what was true at one time was not necessarily true afterward.

There is also the record of laws that have been done away with. The New Testament says of these Old Testament laws:

> Therefore, no one is to act as your judge in regard to food and drink, or in respect to a festival or a new moon, or a Sabbath day-- things which are only a shadow of what is to come; but the substance belongs to Christ (Colossians 2:16,17 NASB 2020).

The interpreter needs to recognize the progressive character of God's revelation. God may add or change certain things He previously revealed.

For example, the Old Testament forbids the people to eat pork. This commandment is rescinded in the New Testament. Paul wrote the following about false teachers who commanded people to abstain from, or not eat, certain foods:

> Now the Spirit expressly says that in latter times some will depart from the faith, giving heed to deceiving spirits and doctrines of demons, speaking lies in hypocrisy, having their own conscience seared with a hot iron, forbidding to marry, *and commanding* to abstain from foods which God created to be received with thanksgiving by those who believe and know the truth (1 Timothy 4:1-3 NKJV).

While Old Testament believers were forbidden to eat certain foods, this is not the case with New Testament believers. Failure to recognize that God has revealed His Word progressively will cause all sorts of problems with interpretation and will cause the reader to assume there are contradictions where there are none.

8. THE BIBLE USES DIFFERENT NAMES FOR THE SAME PEOPLE

Sometimes we find the Bible using a number of different names for the same person. This feature can certainly cause the reader difficulty. In some translations, such as the *King James* Version, the same name is spelled a number of different ways. This can add to the confusion.

9. THERE ARE DIFFERENT METHODS OF CALCULATION

There is also the problem of the biblical writers using different methods of calculating the years. These different methods of calculation can cause apparent discrepancies. It seems that the northern kingdom of

Israel used a different method in calculating the reign of their kings than the southern kingdom of Judah.

10. THE NUMBERS ARE SOMETIMES ROUNDED OFF

When Scripture records numbers, it often rounds them off. Again, we must be careful to understand the author's intent when he gives us a particular number.

Sometimes the number will be exact, but there are other occasions where the writer is speaking in a general manner and rounding off the number—he does not expect the number given to be accepted as the actual amount. Unless this is understood, there will seemingly be a discrepancy.

11. WE MUST DISCOVER WHETHER SOMETHING WAS TOPICAL OR CHRONOLOGICAL

There is also the issue in which the way the material is presented in Scripture. Sometimes a writer follows a more topical outline than a chronological one. This has caused some to believe there is a discrepancy between two accounts.

However, we need to take into consideration the fact that one author may be giving us a chronology of events while another author lists the same events in a topical manner. There is no discrepancy when an author states the same truth as another author but uses a different method in communicating that truth.

12. THERE WAS SELECTIVITY AMONG THE AUTHORS

In addition, each biblical author is selective in the material he records. John made this clear about the gospel he wrote:

> Now Jesus did many other signs in the presence of the disciples, which are not written in this book; but these are written

so that you may believe that Jesus is the Christ, the Son of God, and that by believing you may have life in his name (John 20:30,31 ESV).

From this statement we understand that the author is only giving us a partial report of what he knows to be true.

Therefore, when he records a story about Jesus that is found in another gospel, we should not expect him to tell us every detail that the other gospel writer records. The points that he mentions are those that fit his purpose. The omission of certain details, that other authors may include, does not indicate that he is disagreeing with that author.

13. THE AUTHORS MAY RECORD THE SAME EVENT DIFFERENTLY: IT SHOWS THERE WAS NO COLLUSION

The fact that there are difficulties and apparent contradictions between the authors of the Bible shows there was no collusion among them. Whenever multiple people report an event there will be differences in their accounts—since no two people see everything exactly the same.

Yet those who witness an event will tell the same basic account. The only differences we should expect to find are in the incidental details. This is exactly what we find in Scripture. Differing accounts of the same event are not necessarily false accounts. The difference can simply be one of perspective.

An example of this selectivity is found in the genealogy in Exodus 6:13-27. In this passage only three of the twelve sons of Jacob are listed (Reuben, Simeon, and Levi).

This is because the author's purpose is to emphasize two particular descendants of Levi—Moses and Aaron. Therefore, he goes no further and does not list the other people in the genealogy.

Again, it is the author's purpose in highlighting Moses and Aaron that caused him to stop at Levi when he listed the sons of Jacob.

14. WE MUST DETERMINE WHETHER THE BIBLE IS APPROVING OR MERELY RECORDING THE EVENT

Another concern is determining whether the writer is endorsing a statement, or event, or merely narrating it. Narrating misconduct does not make one responsible for the actions, nor is it an endorsement of that conduct.

There are times in which the Scripture accurately records sinful acts without applauding the deeds. The Bible gives an accurate picture of the lives of its characters, and often this includes recording their evil actions. The life of King David is an example of this. His great deeds of faith are recorded alongside his murder and adultery. The entire picture is given for us with nothing whitewashed.

There are many occasions in Scripture where the author tells what happened without giving any commentary on the matter. Silence should not be regarded as approval. Recording some evil deed is not the same as authorizing it.

Because the Bible does not commend everything that it records, we must always study carefully the context of the particular statement or act. When this is done, many of the problems and difficulties will simply vanish.

Even when interpreted properly, the Bible does contain a number of difficulties. However, these difficulties, once understood, do not prevent the reader from understanding the clear message of Scripture.

SUMMARY TO QUESTION 12
WHAT TYPE OF DIFFICULTIES DO WE FIND IN SCRIPTURE?

There are many areas in Scripture that cause the reader difficulty. These include the following:

The problem of distance between the original authors, and us—at a minimum there has been nineteen hundred years from the last biblical book that was written until today.

The exact meaning of words and phrases also make interpretation difficult. There are also translational misunderstandings that can cause difficulties.

Problems of grammar also complicate proper interpretation. Cultural difficulties can cause problems in interpretation.

Scripture also gives examples of changing historical circumstances. We also find different names used for the same people. Another Bible difficulty is the different methods for calculating years. Numbers in the Scripture are often rounded off. This feature can cause difficulty.

There is also the question of the author narrating in a topical, or chronological, manner. The fact that the authors are selective in what they record also causes difficulty.

Finally, there is the issue of determining whether the author is approving the statement, or event, or merely recording it.

All of these are difficult areas. They must be carefully looked at for a proper understanding of what the biblical author it attempting to say. However, these difficulties do not constitute contradictions. Once understood, these difficulties can be removed, and the text can be accurately interpreted.

How Should Specific Difficulties Be Evaluated?

What should the reader do when they find a difficult passage in the Bible? Is there a way to approach particular problems? The answer is, "Yes." There are several matters that must be kept in mind when one comes across a Bible difficulty.

1. WE SHOULD ASSUME THAT IT WAS WRITTEN TO BE UNDERSTOOD

In assessing any written document, we should always assume that the author had intended to make sense of what he wrote. Therefore, we should use our common sense to understand what the author is trying to say. When someone takes the time to write something, they desire their writing to be understood.

2. WE MUST ASK HOW THE ORIGINAL AUDIENCE WOULD HAVE UNDERSTOOD IT?

The key issue is finding out how the original audience would have understood what was written. What would it have meant to them? This should be our starting point.

3. WE SHOULD GIVE THE BIBLE THE BENEFIT OF THE DOUBT

Whenever a document comes down to us that is reportedly ancient, and it shows no signs of tampering or forgery, and if this document demonstrates that it is correct with the specific references that it gives, then the burden of proof is upon those who doubt its authenticity. The writing in question should always be given the benefit of the doubt.

Therefore, when we meet an apparent "error" in Scripture—a Book that repeatedly has demonstrated itself to be reliable—we should presume the error is because of our ignorance our lack of understanding what the author is saying.

In other words, the Bible *always* gets the benefit of the doubt.

4. WE SHOULD CHECK OUT THE ORIGINAL

Sometimes the problem we face lies in the translation of the passage. When the original language is checked, the discrepancy often goes away. This is why multiple translations of the Bible should be considered when encountering a difficulty.

5. WE MUST LET SCRIPTURE INTERPRET SCRIPTURE

The infallible rule of interpretation of Scripture is the Bible must be allowed to interpret itself. We must remember that the ultimate Author behind each of the books of the Bible is God. When Scripture is compared with Scripture, we can then discover the full implications of what God intended.

6. WE MUST INTERPRET THE OBSCURE BY THE CLEAR

One central rule of interpretation is that we interpret the obscure passage by the clear. We do not try to force the obvious meaning of one text to conform to the obscure meaning of another text. Never should a doctrine be based upon an obscure passage.

A good example of this is 1 Corinthians 15:29. It reads:

Otherwise, what will they do who are baptized for the dead, if the dead do not rise at all? Why then are they baptized for the dead? (1 Corinthians 15:29 NKJV).

We may not exactly know what this passage does mean, but from the totality of Scripture we certainly know what it does not mean. People are not to be baptized in water in place of those who have died.

Another example of making a doctrine out of something obscure would be the "gap theory." This theory, which argues for a gap of time between the first two verses of Genesis, is built upon a questionable translation of the Hebrew. This alone should make the theory suspect.

There is a principle called "the analogy of Scripture." Simply stated, this teaches that every unclear reference should be interpreted in light of something that is clear.

Therefore, we should never assume that an unclear passage contradicts what is clearly taught elsewhere in God's Word, neither should we build any doctrine on some obscure text or translation.

Thus, we should interpret all difficult passages in light of the clear teachings of Scripture. No doctrine should be built upon passages that are obscure. If a certain teaching is vital, then it will be stated in Scripture more than once.

7. WE SHOULD INTERPRET THE BIBLE AS OTHER BOOKS

Another point that needs to be made is that the Bible should be interpreted by the same rules that we use to interpret any other book. There are no special rules we should employ when we interpret the Bible. The Bible should be approached like all other books with regard to interpretation. We should seek to understand how the original readers would have understood it.

8. IT IS IMPORTANT TO LOOK FOR THE LITERAL MEANING

The Bible is God's communication to humanity. Obviously, if the Bible intends to reach the maximum number of people, then the message should be understood at face value. The Bible should be interpreted in a literal manner if at all possible.

A good rule of thumb is this: If the literal sense makes good sense, then seek no other sense, lest you come up with nonsense.

9. WE SHOULD UNDERSTAND DIFFERENT LITERARY DEVICES FOUND IN SCRIPTURE

Sometimes the difficulty we encounter is a result of an incorrect understanding of the type of language the author is employing. The Bible contains different literary styles.

In the pages of Scripture, we find such styles as narrative, law, and poetry. Sometimes the difficulty lies in the incorrect identification of the type of literary form the author is employing.

Literal interpretation allows for figures of speech. The Bible, at times, uses figures of speech to communicate its truth. These figures of speech should not be interpreted in the same way as a simple narration of events. Literal interpretation does not mean that every sentence and every statement must be interpreted literally when the context calls for a non-literal interpretation.

If the Bible is read as other literature, allowing the author to say what he wishes in the different literary forms, then there will be no major problem understanding that which is to be taken literally and that which is meant to be non-literal. It is crucial to understand this.

10. IT IS CRUCIAL TO ALWAYS CHECK OUT THE CONTEXT

The Bible should always be interpreted contextually. This means the context should be studied in order to see how each verse relates to that which precedes and that which follows. Close attention should be paid to the theme and scope of the biblical book under consideration. Context should always be a determining factor when interpreting any difficult passage.

For example, it could be argued that the Bible teaches that God does not exist. Psalm 14:1 says, "there is no God."

By itself, this statement seems to teach atheism. However, the statement is prefaced by this qualification: "The fool says in his heart, 'There is no God.'" Each statement of the Bible needs to be read in its context.

11. WE MUST REALIZE THAT NOT EVERY STATEMENT IS TRUE

When we read the Bible, should we regard every statement as true? Can we confidently read any portion of Scripture, and act upon any statement? The answer is no. A distinction needs to be made between the accuracy of the statements in the Bible, and their truthfulness.

Divine inspiration guarantees the accuracy of every statement, but not the truth of it. For example, every time Satan spoke, he lied. Jesus said of him:

> You belong to your father the devil, and you want to do what he wants. He was a murderer from the beginning and was against the truth, because there is no truth in him. When he tells a lie, he shows what he is really like, because he is a liar and the father of lies. But because I speak the truth, you don't believe me (John 8:44,45 NCV).

In the Garden of Eden, the serpent promised Eve that she and her husband would be like God if they ate of the forbidden fruit. The Bible says:

> The serpent said to the woman, "Surely you will not die, for God knows that when you eat from it your eyes will open

and you will be like divine beings who know good and evil"
(Genesis 3:4,5 NET).

The New International Version translates it this way:

> "You will not surely die," the serpent said to the woman.
> "For God knows that when you eat of it your eyes will be
> opened, and you will be like God, knowing good and evil"
> (Genesis 3:4,5, NIV).

The statement of the serpent is recorded accurately, but the statement
is not true.

Other examples can be found in Scripture where people made statements that are against the clear teaching of God and His Word.

12. THE BIBLE WAS WRITTEN IN NON-TECHNICAL LANGUAGE

It is also important to understand the manner in which the truth is communicated in Scripture. The Bible is written in non-technical language to reach the maximum number of people. Whenever any event occurs, there are two basic ways of explaining it. One way is to give a technical explanation. However, the more technical the language the more limited your audience will be.

A second possible way of explaining things is to relate how the event appears to the observer. It is this non-technical way in which the Bible describes events.

For example, the events of creation recorded in the early chapters of Genesis are not described in terms of modern scientific classification but are described from the vantage point of an observer here on earth.

The Bible does not use the technical language of science, but rather the non-technical language of the marketplace. The biblical writers dealing with concepts of their times used the language of their times. The scriptural language is the language of common everyday use.

Therefore, the words of the Bible are neither scientific, nor unscientific, in nature, but are rather timeless, and non-scientific. The language of Scripture is the language of appearance. Biblical writers describe things as they appear to the observer. This is also known as "phenomenal" language.

Furthermore, the Bible does not attempt to give technical answers to technical questions. Since the Bible speaks in everyday language to all people of all times, it is not correct to look for answers explained in technical scientific language. This type of language soon becomes out of date and would be irrelevant for future generations.

13. OUR INTERPRETATION IS NOT INFALLIBLE

The Bible alone is the inerrant Word of God—not our personal interpretation of it. Unfortunately, there have been mistaken interpretations of the Bible by certain "church" authorities. This has caused some to think the Scripture is in error.

A classic example of this is the mistaken view that the earth is the center of the universe. Because the Bible speaks of things from an earth-centered viewpoint, some have thought Scripture was affirming that the earth, not the sun, was the center of the universe.

This earth-centered idea became an article of faith for many in the church. They attempted to silence those who taught otherwise. Sadly, this was all based upon a wrong interpretation of Scripture.

Therefore, we should not make the mistake of believing that science and the Bible are at odds because of a wrong interpretation of the facts of Scripture. The infallibility is in the Scripture itself, not in our interpretation. When Christians read their own fallible interpretation into Scripture, this does not mean the Bible is in error. Rather, it means the interpreter made a mistake.

14. WHAT ABOUT THE AUTHOR'S INTENT?

One of the ways of understanding any written communication is attempting to find out the author's intent. However, when we come to the Bible, we encounter a number of problems if we attempt to do this. They are as follows.

WE NEED TO REALIZE THE BIBLE HAS DUAL AUTHORSHIP

First, Scripture is clear that it is the result of more than one author. There are the various human authors of Scripture, but ultimately God is behind the wording of Scripture. Therefore, it is not always possible to attempt to discover the author's intent since every part of Scripture is the result of dual authorship. It is divine/human.

WE DO NOT KNOW THE MIND OF GOD UNLESS HE REVEALS IT

As far as God is concerned, we do not know what He is thinking unless He tells us. God has said that His thoughts are beyond our comprehension:

> For my thoughts *are* not your thoughts, neither *are* your ways my ways, saith the LORD. For *as* the heavens are higher than the earth, so are my ways higher than your ways, and my thoughts than your thoughts (Isaiah 55:8,9 KJV).

In addition, we are told that at times the human authors did not realize what they were writing. Peter wrote:

> Concerning this salvation, the prophets who predicted the grace that would come to you searched and investigated carefully. They probed into what person or time the Spirit of Christ in them was indicating when he testified beforehand about the sufferings appointed for Christ and his subsequent glory. They were shown that they were serving not themselves but you, in regard to the things now announced to

you through those who evangelized you by the Holy Spirit sent from heaven—things angels long to catch a glimpse of (1 Peter 1:10-12 NET).

Consequently, since they did not always realize the exact meaning of what they were writing, it is fruitless for us to attempt to discern their intent. All of this makes attempting to find the intent of the author a futile exercise. The best thing to do is try to discover how the original audience would have understood it.

CONCLUSION: THESE FACTS SHOULD BE KEPT IN MIND WHEN BIBLE DIFFICULTIES ARE EXAMINED

If we consider all these facts whenever we encounter a difficulty in Scripture, it will help us in coming to some type of answer to the problem. While not all difficulties have obvious answers to them, we can certainly eliminate a number of difficulties if we apply some of these points.

SUMMARY TO QUESTION 13
HOW SHOULD SPECIFIC DIFFICULTIES IN SCRIPTURE BE EVALUATED?

When one encounters a difficult passage in God's Word the following facts should be considered.

First, we should assume the author wants to make sense. This is true of all authors—they write to be understood.

Second, we should attempt to ascertain how the original readers would understand what the author had written.

In areas of difficulty we should give the Bible the benefit of the doubt. When at all possible, check out the original.

It is also important to realize that Scripture interprets Scripture. It is crucial to interpret the obscure passages by the clear ones.

We must make certain we interpret the Bible as other books. Although one should always look first for the literal meaning, it is also important to realize that the Bible sometimes employs figures of speech.

It is also vital that we make certain that we always check out the context. It is also necessary to realize that not every statement in the Bible is true – just that it is accurately recorded.

Remember, too, that Bible was written in non-technical language. Above all, let us understand that our interpretation is not infallible.

Finally, we should not be overly concerned to attempt to find the authors' intent—seeing that each portion of Scripture has a human and a divine author. It is better to try and understand how the original readers or hearers of the message would have understood it.

What Specific Objections Have Been Made Against The Inerrancy Or The Trustworthiness Of Scripture?

The Christian church has always believed and taught that the Bible is trustworthy in all that it records. All statements found in it are recorded accurately.

Yet, this idea has been met with objections from within and without the Christian community. Unhappily, many people have assumed that these objections cannot be adequately answered.

However, this is not the case. Every objection that has been brought forward against the doctrine of inerrancy has a reasonable answer.

THE MAJOR OBJECTIONS MADE AGAINST AN INERRANT BIBLE

We can list the major objections against an inerrant Bible as follows.

Objection 1: There are demonstrable errors in the Bible.

Objection 2: The discovery of one small error would cause everything to be rejected. Therefore, inerrancy should not be taught.

Objection 3: To be inerrant, everything in the Bible must be understood literally. This would make the Bible absurd.

Objection 4: Certain biblical doctrines which are found in Scripture were changed over time.

Objection 5: Paul made a distinction between his fallible words and those of Jesus.

Objection 6: Inerrancy means exact scientific precision and the Bible does not teach that about itself.

Objection 7: There are grammatical errors in Scripture.

Objection 8: The Bible cannot be inerrant because humans are not.

Objection 9: To communicate with the people, God accommodated Himself to the errors of the times.

Objection 10: The original writings are missing.

Objection 11: There are mistakes in the various copies of Scripture.

Objection 12: Modern science has refuted an inerrant Bible.

Objection 13: The New Testament does not quote the Old Testament word for word.

Objection 14: Inerrancy causes worship of the Bible.

Objection 15: There are too many qualifications to the doctrine of inerrancy.

Objection 16: Many statements in Scripture cannot be proven to be true or false.

Objection 17: No translation of the Bible is perfect. Therefore, the doctrine of inerrancy is irrelevant.

These are the usual objections that are raised when Christians speak of a totally trustworthy, or an inerrant Bible.

Yet, as we shall see, all of these objections have reasonable answers.

Therefore, it is not necessary for anyone to assume that the Bible is a document that contains errors.

SUMMARY TO QUESTION 14
WHAT SPECIFIC OBJECTIONS HAVE BEEN MADE AGAINST THE INERRANCY OR TRUSTWORTHINESS OF SCRIPTURE?

The following seventeen points have been raised against the doctrine of an inerrant, or totally trustworthy, Bible. First, it is argued there are demonstrable errors in the Bible. This should be the end of the story. Also, it is argued that if the doctrine of inerrancy is held, then one small error would cause the entire Christian faith to be rejected.

Others insist that inerrancy means that all Scripture must be interpreted literally. This brings about absurd results. In addition, it is alleged that certain Bible doctrines have been changed over time. This is not consistent with any doctrine of inerrancy. We also find Paul making a distinction between his fallible words, and the words of Jesus.

The fact that inerrancy means exact scientific precision shows the Bible cannot be inerrant because it is not scientifically precise. Add to this the Bible does not clearly teach inerrancy—it is something that is read into Scripture.

There is more. We find grammatical errors in Scripture. How can this come from a perfect God? Moreover, the Bible cannot be inerrant because humans are not. It is admitted by everyone that human beings wrote the books of the Bible.

Since the original writings are missing, how can anyone claim inerrancy for them? Everyone also admits there are mistakes in the various manuscript copies of Scripture. This would prove inerrancy is a myth. Modern science has allegedly refuted an inerrant Bible.

When we examine the New Testament citations of the Old Testament, we find they do not match word for word. This is inconsistent with inerrancy. It is claimed inerrancy causes worship of the Bible instead of the worship of God. Consequently, the doctrine should be discarded.

Furthermore, there are too many qualifications to the doctrine to make it meaningful. There is also the fact that certain portions of the Bible are not relevant to the issue of inerrancy. In addition, no Bible translation is perfect. Therefore, how can anyone speak of an inerrant Bible?

All of these objections have been raised against the idea that the Bible is the error-free revelation of God. It is important to note that all these objections can be reasonably answered if one take the time to thoroughly examine the subject.

QUESTION 15

Aren't There Examples Of Demonstrable Errors In The Bible?

It is claimed that there are clear examples of demonstrable errors in the Bible. This is the real issue in the matter of biblical inerrancy. If a genuine contradiction, or error, can be clearly demonstrated, then the concept of the inerrancy of the Scripture must fall by the wayside. Critics are quick to point out that there are demonstrable errors in Scripture. What are we to make of these accusations?

THERE ARE DIFFICULTIES IN SCRIPTURE NOT ERRORS

We would respond to this charge by admitting there are indeed difficulties in Scripture. However, it is not necessary to conclude that these difficulties are errors. A number of points need to be made about this important issue.

Bible Difficulties In Scripture Fit Into Three Categories

The so-called "errors" in the Bible can be divided into three basic categories. They include the following.

1. SOME DIFFICULTIES ARE DUE TO A MISUNDERSTANDING OF SCRIPTURE

In the first category there is a misunderstanding of what the Bible says or does not say. The error is with the person attributing something to Scripture that is not there.

This could be a problem with the translation or with the understanding of the text as it now stands. When properly translated and understood in context, the supposed error vanishes. This is why we closely need to look at the biblical text.

2. MOST DIFFICULTIES HAVE A LEGITIMATE SOLUTION

There is another category of so-called "errors," which, in actuality, are merely difficulties. At first glance they appear to be errors in Scripture. However, these difficulties have legitimate solutions that can resolve the problem.

It is a basic principle of historical study that if there is a reasonable way of harmonizing two statements, then this should be preferred rather than saying the document is inaccurate or in error. This is true whether the statements are found in the one writer, or in different writers. Consequently, these types of difficulties cannot be called errors if a reasonable solution can be offered.

Furthermore, we should not think that these Bible difficulties have been only recently discovered by modern scholarship. Most Bible difficulties have been recognized from the beginning and have been dealt with long ago by the early Christians. They offered satisfactory solutions to the problems.

3. THERE ARE ONLY A FEW BIBLE DIFFICULTIES THAT PRESENTLY DO NOT HAVE CLEAR SOLUTIONS: IN SOME CASES, WE MUST WAIT AND SEE

There are a small number of places in Scripture where there is presently no clear solution to the difficulty. However, rarely do we find that there is no obvious solution to a biblical problem, or a solution that does not carry conviction. It is mainly these places where critics accuse the Bible of error.

There are few things that need to be said about difficulties in this category.

First, the fact that there is presently no clear solution to a particular difficulty does not mean there will never be a solution. As advances in linguistics, history, and archaeology continue to take place, more and more of the so-called "errors" of Scripture now have plausible solutions.

In almost every case where a so-called "error" is found, there is at least some plausible explanation to the difficulty. The point is that we do not have to commit intellectual suicide by believing in an error-free Bible.

In addition, there have been a number of instances in the past where the Bible was accused of being in error but now it is not. The history of biblical criticism is filled with examples of "proofs" of the inaccuracy of Scripture that were once taken for granted.

However, further knowledge has shown that the error was on the part of the one who criticized the Bible as being untrue—not on the Scripture. Since this has happened so many times in the past no one should be quick to accuse the Scripture of error—especially when it has proved its trustworthiness time and time again.

The point is this: the Bible is academically defensible. The objections that arise to the doctrine of inerrancy can be reasonably answered. A believer does not have to be embarrassed for believing and promoting the inerrancy, or total trustworthiness, of Scripture.

For those few places where no clear solution is presently available, the believer waits for further knowledge to vindicate Scripture. As we have seen so often in the past, further knowledge has erased Bible difficulties time and time again. Therefore, as time goes by, more and more of these types of difficulties will be solved.

THE PROPER ATTITUDE IS ESSENTIAL IN DEALING WITH THESE TYPE OF DIFFICULTIES

The key is to have the proper attitude toward the entire Bible, and the difficulties found within its pages. The acceptance of the doctrine of inerrancy means believers submit themselves to the authority of God's Word. We place our faith in the God of truth who has divinely inspired the Bible. The difficulties in Scripture must be kept in perspective with everything else we know about God and His Word.

Thus, one cannot be under the authority of the Bible and, at the same time, be free to accuse it of error. We should always give the Bible the benefit of the doubt until a demonstrable error can be clearly proved. Therefore, when we encounter an historical or theological problem, we honestly face the problem and do not ignore it but at the same time we do not assume that the Bible is in error.

Unresolved problems still remain but this is all that they are—problems. They are not proof of the inaccuracy of Scripture. What we have today is not proof of error—we have only theories and speculation. This is not the same as evidence. Consequently, believers should not abandon their faith in an inerrant Bible merely because of a few difficulties. The Christian must study the Bible with the belief that it is true in all that it says.

ABRAHAM: AN EXAMPLE OF HOW TO DEAL WITH ALLEGED CONTRADICTIONS IN SCRIPTURE

There is a biblical example that helps us deal with the issue of alleged contradictions in the Word of God. This is found in the life of Abraham. Abraham had been promised that God would give him a son and it would be through that promised son a number of things would be fulfilled. This promise was very specific. The Bible says:

> Then God said, "Yes, but your wife Sarah will bear you a son, and you will call him Isaac. I will establish my covenant with him as an everlasting covenant for his descendants after him" (Genesis 17:19 NIV)

Abraham had God's solemn word about the number of his descendants he would have through his son Isaac. As promised, he and Sarah did have a son and Abraham named him Isaac:

> Abraham gave the name Isaac to the son Sarah bore him (Genesis 21:3 NIV).

However, Abraham was eventually faced with a dilemma. Before Isaac was married and had any children that would fulfill the promises of God, Abraham was told to take Isaac and offer him as a human sacrifice. The Bible says:

> Then God said, "Take your son, your only son, Isaac, whom you love, and go to the region of Moriah. Sacrifice him there as a burnt offering on one of the mountains I will tell you about" (Genesis 22:2 NIV).

Abraham was faced with a seeming contradiction in God's Word.

On the one hand, he was promised that Isaac would be the son through whom a number of specific promises would be fulfilled. Yet, God was now telling Abraham to take the son of promise and put him to death. This commandment that God gave Abraham apparently contradicted His earlier promise.

Abraham had a number of options. He could have ignored God's command to sacrifice Isaac. He may have considered that God was testing him to see if he would use his own powers of reason and sense of morality.

Second, Abraham could have believed that God was lying to him when He made the promises concerning Isaac. It was all a cruel hoax.

Finally, Abraham could have concluded that he did not properly understand either God's original promise or the command to sacrifice Isaac.

However, Abraham did none of these three things. Instead, he trusted God.

THE WAY ABRAHAM RESOLVED THE DIFFICULTY HE HAD

The way in which Abraham resolved this difficulty should be instructive for all of us. He obeyed the Word of God without question.

The writer to the Hebrews says the following of Abraham and his obedience:

> It was by faith that Abraham, when God tested him, offered his son Isaac as a sacrifice. God made the promises to Abraham, but Abraham was ready to offer his own son as a sacrifice. God had said, "The descendants I promised you will be from Isaac." Abraham believed that God could raise the dead, and really, it was as if Abraham got Isaac back from death (Hebrews 11:17-19 NCV).

Abraham did not know how God would resolve these seeming contradictions. Yet, he believed God anyway. While it seemed that it would have been impossible for Isaac to fulfill the promises that God made to Abraham, Abraham still chose to trust God.

If necessary, Abraham believed God would raise Isaac from the dead. Yet, it was not necessary. God stopped Abraham as he was about to offer Isaac as a sacrifice.

Therefore, in the Old Testament character Abraham, we find the example of how to respond to so-called "contradictions" that are found in God's Word. We trust in God and wait for Him to resolve the issue in His good time.

God honored Abraham's faith in the face of a seemingly impossible difficulty. He will also honor our faith when we put our trust in Him when we face supposedly insurmountable difficulties contained within Scripture.

SUMMARY TO QUESTION 15
AREN'T THERE EXAMPLES OF DEMONSTRABLE ERRORS IN THE BIBLE?

It has been alleged that there are obvious errors in the Bible and thus the doctrine of inerrancy is clearly untrue. However, the examples that are usually given are difficulties, not errors.

Furthermore, most difficulties in Scripture have plausible explanations. There are only a few Bible difficulties where no adequate solution is presently known. Again, this does not mean the Scripture is in error—it only means that no reasonable solution is available at the present time.

An example of how to deal with Bible difficulties can be found in the life of Abraham. Abraham was told to take Isaac, the son in whom God made many promises, and offer him as a sacrifice. Abraham obeyed, but God stopped him from sacrificing his son. Abraham's example of faith in the Lord is a model for us all.

In the same manner, when faced with a difficulty where there is no apparent solution for the present, we trust God and wait until an answer is found. As we have discovered in so many instances in the past, these answers do, in fact, come!

Would The Discovery Of One Small Error Cause Everything In Scripture To Be Rejected?

One objection against the doctrine of inerrancy concerns the issue of what a proven error in Scripture would mean. If Christians insist that the Scripture cannot contain any type of error because it comes from a perfect God, then does it mean that the authority of Scripture collapses if an error is found?

Must the authority of Scripture be rejected if there is only one proven error found in its pages?

OBJECTION: WHY FORCE THE BIBLE TO BE PLACED IN SUCH A DIFFICULT POSITION?

Therefore, is it asked, "Aren't Christians needlessly putting too much emphasis on this one doctrine which is not explicitly taught in Scripture?" This is especially true because there are a number of unsolved Bible difficulties that still exist without a clear solution. Why then, should we continue to promote inerrancy?

RESPONSE

A few points need to be made. They are as follows.

WE MUST HAVE THE BIBLICAL VIEWPOINT ON THIS ISSUE

While this is a fair question, it has to be answered by looking at the totality of what the Bible says about itself and about God. The doctrine of inerrancy, while not specifically taught in Scripture, follows logically from what the Bible says about God and His words.

To be consistent, Christians should have the same attitude toward the Scripture as did Christ and His apostles. That attitude was one of "total trust." They never cast doubt on any part of Scripture but rather asserted its truthfulness in all areas in which it spoke. It is clear that Jesus believed the Scripture was without error. It is much better to side with Him on this issue rather than compromising our beliefs to allow mistakes in God's Holy Word.

THE NUMBER OF PROBLEMS IS NOT THAT LARGE

While there are some difficulties in the biblical text where there is no clear solution at the present, it must be emphasized that the number of these problems is relatively small when we reflect on the size and scope of Scripture. In fact, when we consider that the Bible was written from two thousand to three thousand four hundred years ago by forty different human authors, we would expect innumerable problems with the text. Yet this is not the case. The number of problems, relatively speaking, is quite small.

ONE ERROR MAY MEAN THERE ARE OTHERS

There is something else that is important to note. While one proven error in Scripture would not necessarily mean that there *are* other errors in Scripture, what it would mean is that there *may* be other errors in Scripture.

Once a person has admitted that an error exists in a certain place in the Bible, then the rest of Scripture comes under suspicion. It would remove certainty from the Bible. Nobody could be confident that any given passage in Scripture was absolutely trustworthy.

THERE ARE NO ERRORS THAT HAVE BEEN PROVEN

We again emphasize that there are no such things as proven errors in Scripture. There are difficulties that have solutions and other difficulties that await solutions.

Yet these difficulties are not the same thing as errors. Furthermore, since the Bible has demonstrated its truthfulness time and time again, and because the claims of Scripture come from the God of truth, it is better to continue to insist that the doctrine of an inerrant Scripture is the only one that fits all the facts.

SUMMARY TO QUESTION 16
WOULD THE DISCOVERY OF ONE SMALL ERROR CAUSE EVERYTHING IN SCRIPTURE TO BE REJECTED?

While it seems that Christians have tried to make too much out of the doctrine of inerrancy, they are only being consistent with what the Bible says about itself and God.

Since Christ and His apostles had a high view of the nature of Scripture, so should believers. Anything less does not do justice to what the Bible says about itself.

In addition, not only are there no proven errors in Scripture, the Bible has demonstrated time and time again that it is accurate in the face of accusations against it.

Therefore, to be consistent, the believer should embrace the doctrine of inerrancy as the only one that makes sense out of the totality of the biblical data.

Does Inerrancy Mean Everything In Scripture Must Be Understood Literally?

One of the objections against inerrancy is the assumption that everything in the Bible must be interpreted in a literal manner. To be inerrant, it is argued, the Scripture must always be understood literally. When one attempts to do this it soon becomes apparent that this will not work. The following examples are usually given.

Was Judah was actually born from a lion? We read the following in the Book of Genesis:

> You are a lion's cub, O Judah; you return from the prey, my son. Like a lion he crouches and lies down, like a lioness-- who dares to rouse him? (Genesis 49:9 NIV).

Did the Red Sea part when God blew His nose? Moses wrote:

> By the blast of your nostrils the waters piled up. The surging waters stood firm like a wall; the deep waters congealed in the heart of the sea (Exodus 15:8 NIV).

Did Jesus teach us to hate our parents? Luke records Him saying the following:

> Whoever comes to me and does not hate father and mother, wife and children, brothers and sisters, yes, and even life itself, cannot be my disciple (Luke 14:26 NRSV).

Are believers supposed to be cannibals? John's gospel says:

> The Jews then disputed among themselves, saying, "How can this man give us his flesh to eat?" So Jesus said to them, "Very truly, I tell you, unless you eat the flesh of the Son of Man and drink his blood, you have no life in you" (John 6:52-53 NRSV).

Supposedly those who believe the Bible is inerrant must understand all these statements, as well as every other statement in Scripture, in a literal manner. How do we respond to this?

LITERAL INTERPRETATION IS NOT ALWAYS NECESSARY

This often-brought-up objection has no basis in fact. It is ridiculous to argue that to believe in inerrancy we must assume that every statement in Scripture must be understood in a literal manner. When Christians say they interpret the Bible literally this does not mean that they do not recognize that the Bible contains figures of speech.

THE BIBLE ALLOWS FOR FIGURES OF SPEECH

Believers understand that there are a number of different types of literary forms in Scripture. For example, the Bible contains parables—earthly stories with a heavenly meaning.

By definition, the parable is not attempting to relay some event that actually occurred. However, the meaning of the parable contains actual, or literal, truth. Truth can be conveyed in a number of literary forms.

Thus, the Bible, like other writings, should have the freedom to convey truth in the various forms that the author wishes to use. The issue is this: Does the Bible contain literal truth? The issue is not: Does the Bible always have to be interpreted in a literal manner?

The key is to find out what the author intended to say, and how his audience would have understood it. We should not presume the author, as well as the audience, understood certain statements to be literal when the literal sense is absurd. The Bible contains spiritual truth in the various literary forms in which it is written.

Therefore, when we come across a statement in Scripture where the literal meaning would result in an obvious error, or it would be inconsistent with what has been revealed elsewhere in the Bible, or would make the passage nonsensical, then another type of interpretation should be found.

SUMMARY TO QUESTION 17
DOES THE DOCTRINE OF INERRANCY MEAN THAT EVERYTHING IN SCRIPTURE SHOULD BE UNDERSTOOD LITERALLY?

While it is often contended that inerrancy, of necessity, means that everything in Scripture must be understood literally, this is not the case. It is recognized that the writers of Scripture employed figures of speech, and their readers would have understood that certain statements were not meant to be understood in a literal manner.

The Bible uses a number of different literary forms and these forms need to be read and understood in the context in which they were given. This is consistent with the doctrine of inerrancy.

Did Certain Bible Doctrines Change Over Time?

One of the arguments against the inerrancy of Scripture is the alleged change of doctrine that takes place over time. Certain writers and biblical characters supposedly changed their beliefs later in their life. This change is not compatible with an inerrant Bible.

ALLEGED EXAMPLES OF CHANGING DOCTRINES

The following examples are usually given of the Scripture changing over time.

JESUS' STATEMENT OF HAVING MORE TO SAY

At the end of Jesus' ministry with His disciples, the Lord told them that He still had more to say to them. On the night of His betrayal He said the following:

> I have much more to say to you, more than you can now bear (John 16:12 NIV).

This supposedly implies that Jesus had changed His mind on some things.

However, this is not the case. Jesus made this statement before His death, resurrection, and ascension. The things He had to tell them could only come about *after* His death and resurrection. He could not explain the meaning of these events until they occurred.

Therefore, we have no change of beliefs—only the statement that He has more to tell them.

PAUL SEEMINGLY CHANGE HIS MIND ABOUT THE COMING OF THE LORD

In his earlier letters, First and Second Thessalonians and First Corinthians, Paul emphasized the soon coming of Jesus Christ to the earth.

However, in his later letters this emphasis is not there. This has caused some to argue that Paul eventually changed his mind and corrected himself about the timing of the coming of the Lord.

Yet, in his later writings Paul does not deny the soon coming of Christ. His later writings were written about different themes. Paul was dealing with situations that had arisen in the churches and his letters addressed these specific issues.

In the final chapter of the last letter that he wrote, we have the statement of Paul as to his hope in Christ. He wrote:

> For I am already being poured out as a drink offering, and the time of my departure is at hand. I have fought the good fight, I have finished the race, I have kept the faith. Finally, there is laid up for me the crown of righteousness, which the Lord, the righteous Judge, will give to me on that Day, and not to me only but also to all who have loved His appearing (2 Timothy 4:6–8 NKJV).

Obviously, Paul had not lost hope in the coming of Christ.

THE PROGRESS OF DOCTRINE IS IGNORED

This objection ignores the progress of doctrine. God did not reveal everything to humanity at once. His revelation was progressive in nature. These earlier revelations were not complete.

Accordingly, the later revelations expanded upon what had earlier been revealed. The progress of doctrine does not imply that the earlier and partial revelations of God were incorrect. There is no contradiction between them.

Therefore, the idea that some of the main characters in the Bible had changed their minds on particular issues has no basis in fact.

SUMMARY TO QUESTION 18
DID CERTAIN BIBLE DOCTRINES CHANGE THROUGH TIME?

It has been alleged that the writers, and main characters, of the Bible changed their beliefs over time. Examples given include Jesus telling His disciples that He had much more to say to them and Paul supposedly changing his belief that Christ was going to return soon.

These examples, however, do not prove any change in their teaching. There is no contradiction concerning what Jesus said to His disciples. Jesus never said that the things He had earlier taught his disciples were wrong—He said that He still had more to teach them. There is no change of beliefs.

There is no contradiction with Paul's early and later ministry. Paul had different subjects to write about later in his ministry. He dealt with details regarding the smooth functioning of the church. The return of Christ was not at issue. Indeed, that subject had already been dealt with.

Furthermore, in the last chapter of his last letter, 2 Timothy, Paul wrote that he was looking for of the Second Coming of Christ.

Therefore, this argument against inerrancy, that certain key figures changed their beliefs over time, has no basis in fact.

Did Paul Make A Distinction Between His Words And the Lord's Words? (1 Corinthians 7:12)

Supposedly, Paul made a clear distinction between his words and the words of the Lord. This, it is argued, demonstrated that Paul did not consider his words to have the same authority as Jesus.

We read the following in his first letter to the Corinthians:

> To the rest I say—I and not the Lord (1 Corinthians 7:12 NRSV).

This statement supposedly shows that Paul did not believe that he had the same authority as Jesus. Does this not prove that his words should be considered as fallible?

THE ISSUE IS WHO SPOKE ON THE SUBJECT

Paul does make a distinction between his words and the words of Jesus. However, this distinction was not in the area of whose words were authoritative—it is a distinction concerning which authoritative teacher spoke on this particular issue.

JESUS DID NOT DIRECTLY SPEAK ON THIS SUBJECT

In context, Paul is dealing with a number of issues regarding marriage. He makes the statement that these words are his, and not that of the

Lord Jesus. He does this because Jesus did not directly comment upon this matter while here upon the earth.

Since Jesus left no divinely authoritative word upon the subject, it was up to the Apostle Paul to give God's Word on these issues. Paul is not comparing the authority of Jesus' words with his own authority to teach. He is merely saying that Jesus did not comment on this matter.

PAUL'S COMMANDS WERE AUTHORITATIVE

After making this statement, Paul then gave some specific commands to the believers concerning how to act in these issues regarding marriage. They are as follows:

> Now, I will speak to the rest of you, though I do not have a direct command from the Lord. If a Christian man has a wife who is an unbeliever and she is willing to continue living with him, he must not leave her. And if a Christian woman has a husband who is an unbeliever, and he is willing to continue living with her, she must not leave him. For the Christian wife brings holiness to her marriage, and the Christian husband brings holiness to his marriage. Otherwise, your children would not have a godly influence, but now they are set apart for him. (But if the husband or wife who isn't a Christian insists on leaving, let them go. In such cases the Christian husband or wife is not required to stay with them, for God wants his children to live in peace.) (1 Corinthians 7:12-15 NLT).

Therefore, Paul is making a strong claim of his own authority. Since he did not have a direct word from the Lord Jesus, he felt he could give his own authoritative word. Later, in the same chapter, he claimed that his commands were authoritative:

> Now regarding your question about the young women who are not yet married. I do not have a command from

the Lord for them. But the Lord in his mercy has given me wisdom that can be trusted, and I will share it with you (1 Corinthians 7:25 NLT).

Basically, Paul is saying the following: since he did not have any authoritative teaching on the subject by Jesus then he would give his own authoritative words. There is no thought here of claiming less authority than Jesus.

Therefore, we have no contradiction between Jesus and Paul. Neither do we have Paul acknowledging his writings were of lesser authority.

SUMMARY TO QUESTION 19
DID PAUL MAKE A DISTINCTION BETWEEN HIS WORDS AND THE LORD'S WORDS? (1 CORINTHIANS 7:12)

Some object to the doctrine of inerrancy by assuming Paul contrasted his words with those of Jesus. While Paul did make a distinction between his words and those of Jesus, it was not in the area of who had authority and who did not.

Paul merely stated that he was giving his authoritative word on certain issues regarding marriage because Jesus did not directly speak about the subject. He was not denying that his commands were any less authoritative. Therefore, there is no contradiction here.

Since The Term "Inerrancy" Means Scientific Precision, Does The Bible Really Teach Inerrancy?

Critics of the doctrine of inerrancy say the term is a poor description of what the Bible says about itself. Since the word "inerrancy" means something that is absolutely scientifically precise, the term does not accurately reflect the teaching of Scripture.

Because the Bible speaks in non-scientific language and often rounds off its numbers, it cannot be inerrant in that sense of the term. Why say the Scriptures are inerrant when the Bible does not? Claiming the Bible is inerrant says more than the Bible itself. It actually adds something to Scripture that is not there.

The response to this argument is as follows.

INERRANCY HAS BEEN CLEARLY DEFINED: IT DOES NOT MEAN SCIENTIFIC PRECISION

Bible students have used the term "inerrancy" to describe the nature of Scripture for about one hundred years. In that time, the doctrine has been clearly defined as well as qualified. When the term has been used to refer to Scripture, it has never been defined in this strict scientific sense.

While inerrancy can mean strict scientific precision in some contexts, it does not follow that it cannot have limitations in meaning in other contexts. Therefore, the argument that "inerrancy" is a poor term with respect to what the Bible teaches about itself does not have much weight.

INERRANCY MAY NOT BE THE BEST TERM AVAILABLE

Inerrancy may not be the best term available. However, it has been in use for one hundred years and will remain in use for years to come. The real issue is not of the definition of this particular term. The real issue is, "Does the Bible always speak the truth?" The term, or terms, that we use about the Bible describing itself is not the main issue.

It is proper for people to use other terms in describing the nature of Scripture. These terms include the following: absolutely trustworthy, infallible, truth without any error, and completely accurate.

THE BIBLE DOES TEACH INERRANCY

While the Bible does not use the word inerrancy in describing itself, the teaching of inerrancy is contained within Scripture. The Scripture claims to be the Word of God, and the Word of God is always true. The logical conclusion to this is that the Bible is without error. Otherwise, one would have to argue that parts of the Scripture are God-inspired error! This would be nonsense.

IT IS KEEPING WITH GOD'S CHARACTER

Inerrancy is in keeping with the perfect character of God. The Bible says that God is true. Paul wrote to the Romans:

> What if some were unfaithful? Will their faithlessness nullify
> the faithfulness of God? By no means! Although everyone is
> a liar, let God be proved true (Romans 3:3,4 NRSV).

If the entire Scripture has God's character and authority behind it, then the Bible, being the product of God's revelation of Himself, must also be true in everything that it says. The psalmist wrote:

> The sum of your word is truth; and every one of your righteous ordinances endures forever (Psalm 119:160 NRSV).

Since the totality of God's Word is truth, we assume that it is without error.

MANY CENTRAL TEACHINGS OF SCRIPTURE INVOLVE ACTUAL HISTORICAL EVENTS THAT MUST HAVE HAPPENED

The Bible deals with the way God has acted in history. Many of the great teachings of Scripture are based upon historical events. These include such as the virgin birth, death, and resurrection of Jesus. Therefore, the truth of these events cannot be overlooked. They must have happened exactly as the Bible says that they happened.

SUMMARY TO QUESTION 20
SINCE THE TERM "INERRANCY" MEANS EXACT SCIENTIFIC PRECISION, DOES THE BIBLE REALLY TEACH INERRANCY?

The word "inerrancy" is not found in Scripture. No one denies this. This has caused some to discard the doctrine. They allege that it is not biblical. It is further argued that people are adding to Scripture by claiming it to be inerrant. Why defend something that the Bible does not teach?

Furthermore, the word "inerrancy" has the idea of exact scientific precision. The Bible does not teach that about itself. Therefore, the term should be abandoned.

However, no responsible Bible teacher, who has defined inerrancy with respect to what the Scripture says, has argued for exact scientific precision. Inerrancy, when referring to the Bible, is defined as a work that does not contain errors of any sort—whether it be theological, historical, or scientific. Nothing is claimed with respect to scientific precision. Therefore, the term is consistent with this definition.

While the word "inerrancy" is nowhere found in Scripture the idea is certainly there. The fact that God is perfect, and that the Bible comes from this perfect God, makes the belief in inerrancy a logical conclusion. Otherwise, one would have to argue that the Bible contains God-inspired errors. This idea is contradictory to the very nature of God.

Are There Grammatical Errors In Scripture?

One of the arguments brought forth against an inerrant Bible concerns errors of grammar in the text. Since the language of Scripture does not always conform to the normal rules of grammar, it is assumed to be in error in those particular instances. A number of examples are usually given.

1. THERE ARE EXAMPLES OF GRAMMATICAL IRREGULARITIES

There are a number of examples of grammatical irregularities in Scripture. This is especially true in the Book of Revelation.

John, the author of this book, often uses a plural verb when the accepted practice was to use a singular verb. These are known as solecisms.

John also used an ungrammatical construction in describing Jesus. He wrote the following:

> John to the seven churches that are in Asia: Grace to you and peace from him who is and who was and who is to come, and from the seven spirits who are before his throne (Revelation 1:4 NRSV).

The words, "From him who is, and who was, and who is to come" are written in very ungrammatical Greek.

Other illustrations can be given where standard grammar is not used. For example, Paul begins the third chapter of Ephesians by using a sentence that does not have a verb. This is not correct grammar.

In addition, Jesus, in describing His Person and ministry, used mixed metaphors by referring to Himself as both a door and a shepherd. What are we to make of things such as these?

RESPONSE

The response to this type of objection is as follows.

A. GRAMMATICAL DIFFICULTIES ARE NOT THE ISSUE FOR BIBLICAL INERRANCY

Whether or not certain sentences in Scripture conform to the accepted grammatical usage at that time, or in our time, is not really the issue. Someone can make a true statement that is considered to be ungrammatical.

In addition, someone else can use absolutely perfect grammar in the process of telling untruths. The real issue is, "Does the author tell the truth?" In other words, does what is said mislead the reader? It is not, "Does the author use correct grammar?"

B. WHO SAYS WHAT CORRECT GRAMMAR IS?

There is also the issue of who is to say what is, or what is not, correct grammar. There is no such thing as a "grammatical Bible" that tells everyone exactly how people *must* express themselves in writing. Grammar simply describes how a particular society has spoken and written at a particular time in history. Over time, grammatical rules change.

There is something else that needs to be considered. Many modern authors will use a grammatical construction that is considered outside the realm of normal usage. The author does this to bring about some special affect.

Since this is often practiced today, why shouldn't it be allowed in Scripture? Therefore, the use, or non-use, of certain grammatical features is not the issue that we should be concerned with. The question that has to be answered is, "Did the writers tell the truth?"

C. REVELATION 1:4 HAS A UNIQUE EMPHASIS

With respect to Revelation 1:4, John purposefully uses non-standard grammar to emphasize the nature of God. He is the one who exists, who has existed, and who will exist in the future. While the verse may be grammatically awkward, what it says about the nature of God is absolutely true and quite profound.

CONCLUSION: THE ISSUE IS THE TRUTH OF THE BIBLE, NOT WHETHER THE GRAMMAR IS ALWAYS IN ACCORD WITH SOME STANDARD

Therefore, we conclude the doctrine of inerrancy is not refuted by grammatical irregularities in Scripture. Again, the issue is, "Does the Bible tell the truth?" The totality of the evidence shows that indeed it does.

SUMMARY TO QUESTION 21
ARE THERE GRAMMATICAL ERRORS IN SCRIPTURE?

While there may be some parts of Scripture that do not conform to what was the accepted means of writing in that day, this really does not have any bearing on the inerrancy of Scripture. The key issue is whether or not the Bible speaks truth—not whether correct grammar is always used.

Indeed, there is really no such thing as correct, or incorrect, grammar in the sense that it has unbreakable rules.

Did God Accommodate Himself To The Ignorance Of The Times? (The Accommodation Theory)

There are some people who assume the Scripture teaches the eternal truths of God, but that there are errors in subjects which are not dealing with *spiritual* truth. This is because the purpose of Scripture is only to teach God's truth, not truth on other subjects.

ACCUSATION: GOD ALLOWED ERRORS IN SCRIPTURE BECAUSE HE WAS ONLY TEACHING SPIRITUAL TRUTH

This view says that God communicated His truth through Scripture, but in doing so He did not correct the faulty scientific and historical beliefs of the people. This includes such things as believing in the devil and demons, special creation instead of evolution, and certain events recorded in the Old Testament.

Instead of correcting all the untruths that the people in the biblical times believed, God merely taught them His truth, and let them assume their unscientific and unhistorical views were correct.

Since it would have been difficult for the authors of Scripture to correct so many misunderstandings of fact, God decided to leave them ignorant of these things. This view is also known as the "accommodation theory." Consequently, what we have in the Bible is God's truth mixed with scientific and historical errors.

RESPONSE TO THE ACCOMMODATION THEORY

There are a number of objections to this way of thinking.

WHERE ARE THE ERRORS IN SCRIPTURE?

The first objection to this view is the assumption that there are errors in Scripture. The consistent theme of the Bible is that the written Scriptures are God's Words, and that God does not lie. The objector must first demonstrate even minor errors of history and science. This has not been done. Therefore, the theory is unnecessary.

IF HE ACCOMMODATED HIS WORDS THEN HE IS NO LONGER THE GOD OF TRUTH

There is a greater problem with this theory. If God spoke untruths to humanity, for whatever reason, then He would no longer be the God who does not lie. However, Scripture emphasizes that He is the God who always tells the truth. Paul wrote:

> This letter is from Paul, a slave of God and an apostle of Jesus Christ. I have been sent to bring faith to those God has chosen and to teach them to know the truth that shows them how to live godly lives. This truth gives them the confidence of eternal life, which God promised them before the world began—and he cannot lie (Titus 1:1,2 NLT).

According to the Apostle, Paul the God of the Bible does not lie. In fact, Paul says that He cannot lie! The fact that God cannot and does not lie is in conflict with the idea that He accommodated Himself to the ignorant beliefs at the time.

The writer to the Hebrews stated it this way:

> When people take an oath, they call on someone greater than themselves to hold them to it. And without any question

that oath is binding. God also bound himself with an oath, so that those who received the promise could be perfectly sure that he would never change his mind. So God has given us both his promise and his oath. These two things are unchangeable because it is impossible for God to lie. Therefore, we who have fled to him for refuge can take new courage, for we can hold on to his promise with confidence (Hebrews 6:16-18 NLT).

According to this theory, God intentionally lied to humanity. Yet, this is completely contrary to His moral character. Indeed, God cannot be the God of truth and, at the same time, lie to His people.

Therefore, His character is at stake in this matter as to whether He did, or did not, accommodate His words to the ignorance of the day. Did He tell the truth or did He lie?

JESUS WAS NOT AFRAID TO POINT OUT ERROR

There is something else that we must appreciate. Jesus did not hesitate to expose error and sinful behavior. We can give a number of examples of this from the New Testament. They include the following.

JESUS DROVE OUT THE MONEYCHANGERS FROM THE TEMPLE

Jesus chased the moneychangers away from the temple area. John records the following response of the Lord Jesus to the corruption He found in the temple:

Making a whip of cords, he drove all of them out of the temple, both the sheep and the cattle. He also poured out the coins of the money changers and overturned their tables. He told those who were selling the doves, "Take these things out of here! Stop making my Father's house a marketplace!" (John 2:15,16 NRSV).

Jesus certainly did not hesitate to right a wrong when necessary.

JESUS CORRECTED NICODEMUS

Jesus corrected Nicodemus—a leading Jewish teacher. When Nicodemus asked Jesus a question, Jesus responded in the following manner:

> Are you the teacher of Israel and yet you don't understand these things? (John 3:10 NET).

Jesus had no problem correcting Nicodemus.

HE WARNED OF FALSE PROPHETS

Jesus warned of false prophets that would come in the midst of believers. In the Sermon on the Mount, we read the following:

> Beware of false prophets, who come to you in sheep's clothing but inwardly are ravenous wolves (Matthew 7:15 NRSV).

This warning makes it clear that some people, who claim to teach God's truth, are not really doing so.

JESUS CORRECTED UNBIBLICAL TRADITIONS

Jesus rebuked those who held traditions that were contrary to the Word of God.

In Matthew's gospel, we read of the following encounter of Jesus with the religious leaders:

> Then Pharisees and scribes came to Jesus from Jerusalem and said, "Why do your disciples break the tradition of the elders? For they do not wash their hands before they eat." He answered them, "And why do you break the commandment of God for the sake of your tradition?" (Matthew 15:1-3 NRSV).

These traditions were actually contradicting the things God had previously revealed. Jesus had no problem correcting them.

JESUS REBUKED THE SADDUCEES FOR THEIR UNDERSTANDING OF SCRIPTURE

Jesus told the Sadducees that they did not understand the Scripture, nor the power of God. We read in Matthew:

> But Jesus answered and said to them, "You are mistaken, since you do not understand the Scriptures nor the power of God" (Matthew 22:29 NASB 2020).

This is a strong statement of Jesus. He let them know about these two subjects in which they were ignorant.

JESUS REBUKED THE RELIGIOUS LEADERS FOR THEIR BEHAVIOR

Jesus called the religious leaders of His day, "blind guides." He said:

> Woe to you, blind guides, who say, 'Whoever swears by the temple, that is nothing; but whoever swears by the gold of the temple is obligated' (Matthew 23:16 NET).

On the other hand, Jesus commended those who answered correctly. To a young ruler who was asking about eternal life, we read the following from Jesus:

> And He [Jesus] said to him, "You have answered rightly; do this and you will live" (Luke 10:28 NKJV).

Consequently, there is nothing in the life or ministry of Jesus that would give us the slightest hint that He accommodated Himself to wrong beliefs rather than correct His ignorant contemporaries.

SHOULD WE IMITATE A GOD WHO LIES?

The final problem with this perspective is that we would be commanded to imitate a God who lies, or who tells half-truths. Scripture says that we should imitate God's character:

> You shall not make yourselves abominable with any creeping thing that creeps; nor shall you make yourselves unclean with them, lest you be defiled by them. 'For I *am* the LORD your God. You shall therefore consecrate yourselves, and you shall be holy; for I am holy. Neither shall you defile yourselves with any creeping thing that creeps on the earth' (Leviticus 11:43,44 NKJV).

Jesus said:

> But why do you call Me 'Lord, Lord,' and do not do the things which I say? (Luke 6:36 NKJV).

However, if the accommodation theory is true, then God purposely made some false statements in Scripture to more effectively communicate with humanity.

Therefore, it would not be sinful for us to do the same thing. In fact, we would be *commanded* to do this because we are to imitate God!

Such an idea is totally foreign to all of Scripture. Paul wrote that believers are to put away lies and speak the truth:

> Put on your new nature, created to be like God—truly righteous and holy. So stop telling lies. Let us tell our neighbors the truth, for we are all parts of the same body (Ephesians 4:24-25 NLT).

Therefore, the accommodation theory is totally contrary to what Scripture says about the character and commands of God. Consequently, it should be soundly rejected.

SUMMARY TO QUESTION 22
DID GOD ACCOMMODATE HIMSELF TO THE IGNORANCE OF THE TIMES?
(THE ACCOMMODATION THEORY)

The accommodation theory says that God did not attempt to correct the faulty scientific beliefs that were held in biblical times. Rather, He accommodated Himself to these incorrect historical, spiritual, and unscientific beliefs of the people.

It was not His purpose to teach people about the functioning of the universe—it was to teach them spiritual truth. Therefore, we should expect to find historical and scientific errors in Scripture.

However, this theory does not really take into account what the Bible says about itself. The Bible claims to be God's truth to humanity. It makes no distinction between the spiritual, historical, and the scientific.

Furthermore, this theory assumes errors in Scripture. This is an assumption that still needs to be proved. Until it is proven, then it is not necessary to assume God accommodated Himself to the superstitions that were held by the people.

There are other problems. As we see from the New Testament, Jesus was not afraid to rebuke error whenever He found it. There are a number of examples of Him, found in the four gospels, where the Lord corrected the errors of the people.

Consequently, we should assume the truthfulness of statements that He did not correct.

In sum, the totality of Scripture is against any idea of God accommodating Himself to the ignorant and unscientific views of the people.

How Can The Bible Be Inerrant Since Human Beings Are Not?

One objection that always arises against the doctrine of the inerrancy of the Bible is our human nature. It is the nature of human beings to make mistakes. There are no exceptions.

Since human beings wrote the Bible, and human beings always make mistakes, then we should expect the Bible to contain mistakes. Therefore, it is nonsense to speak of an inerrant Bible.

Although this is a common argument, it has a number of fallacies.

THE AUTHORSHIP OF SCRIPTURE WAS HUMAN AND DIVINE

While acknowledging that human beings did write the Scripture, there is also the divine side to the authorship. While human beings may lie, God does not lie. Moses wrote:

> God is not man, that he should lie, or a son of man, that he should change his mind. Has he said, and will he not do it? Or has he spoken, and will he not fulfill it? (Numbers 23:19 ESV).

The New Revised Standard Version translates the verse in this manner:

God is not a human being, that he should lie, or a mortal, that he should change his mind. Has he promised, and will he not do it? Has he spoken, and will he not fulfill it? (Numbers 23:19 NRSV).

Since God was behind the composition of the biblical books, they cannot contain mistakes. Otherwise, we would be left with God-inspired error! Such a concept is nonsense.

HUMANS DO NOT HAVE TO MAKE MISTAKES

There is another objection to this view. While humans do make mistakes, they do not have to make mistakes. The point is this: Human beings can perform acts that are mistake free.

For example, a person can copy a page of printed text in his or her own handwriting without making any mistakes. Merely because the person is human does not mean that they have to make mistakes in copying the words.

Also, a person can take a test and get every answer correct. The fact of their humanity does not stop them from getting all of the answers right. Examples like this can be multiplied. It should be obvious that while humans do make mistakes, it is not necessary to conclude that there will be mistakes in everything that they do.

Consequently, it is certainly possible that the Bible could have been written in an error-free manner.

ADAM AND EVE WERE HUMAN BEFORE THEY SINNED

Furthermore, if humans always have to make mistakes, then Adam and Eve would not have been considered human until they sinned. Yet the Bible says they were fully human before they sinned. Not only were they fully human, they were perfect in all their behavior until they sinned.

JESUS WAS FULLY HUMAN AND HE NEVER MADE MISTAKES

In addition, we have the example of Jesus. Jesus was fully human, yet He did not sin. The writer to the Hebrews testified:

> For we do not have a high priest who is unable to sympathize with our weaknesses, but we have one who in every respect has been tested as we are, yet without sin. Let us therefore approach the throne of grace with boldness, so that we may receive mercy and find grace to help in time of need (Hebrews 4:15,16 NRSV).

While human beings can and do sin, they do not always have to sin or make mistakes. This point must be remembered.

GOD USED HIS PROVIDENTIAL CARE IN PRESERVING SCRIPTURE

In addition, the Bible itself testifies that God providentially supervised the writers of Scripture to record exactly what He wanted to be recorded. Jesus promised that the Holy Spirit would supernaturally guide His disciples. He promised:

> But the Advocate, the Holy Spirit, whom the Father will send
> in my name, will teach you everything, and will cause you to
> remember everything I said to you (John 14:26 NET).

Therefore, the appeal to mistake-prone human nature is not a valid objection against inerrancy. Humans can perform error-free acts and the Bible is an example of human beings, along with God's divine inspiration, producing an error-free book. There is nothing irrational or illogical about God doing this. In fact, nothing is too difficult for the God of the Bible.

The prophet Jeremiah records the Lord saying the following:

> Behold, I *am* the LORD, the God of all flesh: is there any
> thing too hard for me? (Jeremiah 32:27 KJV).

The answer is "No." There is nothing too difficult for the Lord. Therefore, God is certainly able to preserve His word in an error-free manner.

While errors and untruths characterize human speech, God's speech is entirely different. This is true even when it is spoken through sinful, fallible human beings—it is never false. It is crucial, therefore, for us to realize that God speaking through humans is unlike ordinary human speech.

THE WRITERS WERE KEPT FROM ERROR ONLY IN THEIR TEACHING AND WRITING

There is an important distinction that has to be made. The authors of Scripture were kept from error in everything that they wrote. In addition, the prophets of God spoke God's truth without error.

However, this does not mean they were kept from error in everything they taught and believed.

For example, most if not all of Jesus' disciples, unless otherwise instructed, would probably have believed that the earth was flat. The biblical characters would have held the common beliefs of people of their time. This is, of course, unless God directly revealed something that was contrary to the prevailing belief.

The point is that the biblical authors were fallible human beings who made mistakes and were ignorant in certain beliefs. However, they were kept from error in those things which they spoke or wrote with the Lord's authority. This is because the Holy Spirit supernaturally kept them from error and guided them into all truth. This is a crucial distinction.

We find an example of this in the life of the prophet Nathan. The Bible says the following:

King David moved into his new palace, and the Lord let his kingdom be at peace. Then one day, as David was talking with Nathan the prophet, David said, "Look around! I live in a palace made of cedar, but the sacred chest has to stay in a tent." Nathan replied, "The Lord is with you, so do what you want!" (2 Samuel 7:1-3 CEV).

The prophet Nathan told David to go ahead and build a temple for the Lord because the Lord was with him. However, that night the Lord appeared to Nathan and told him that He did not authorize David to build a temple for him. Nathan then went to David with the words that the Lord had revealed to him:

According to all these words and according to all this vision, so Nathan spoke to David (2 Samuel 7:17 NKJV).

This teaches several important truths. First, a prophet was not infallible in everything that he or she said. They were only infallible when the Lord directed their words. They would preface these words with phrases such as, "Thus says the Lord."

If, like Nathan, they presumed to speak for the Lord when the Lord had not directed them, they would be corrected. This assures us that on other occasions, when the prophets spoke, and their words were recorded and not corrected, that they were indeed speaking for the Lord.

The God of the Bible is the Lord of everything, including human language. This being the case, He is certainly able to supervise the writing of Scripture to bring the desired result He wants.

Consequently, everything in Scripture that is prefaced with "thus says the Lord" can be accepted as absolutely true.

SUMMARY TO QUESTION 23
HOW CAN THE BIBLE BE INERRANT SINCE HUMAN BEINGS ARE NOT?

Inerrancy is often assumed to be impossible because of the nature of human beings. Since human beings are fallible, and humans wrote the Bible, then, it is argued, the Bible must be fallible.

This, however, is a fallacy. While it is true that humans are fallible, they can perform error-free acts. While humans can and do make mistakes, they do not always have to.

It is possible for humans to compose a book that is correct in everything that it states—particularly when the Holy Spirit is guiding the things that are being written.

This objection also overlooks the divine side of Scripture. God supernaturally preserved the biblical writers from error. Consequently, the fact that humans were involved in the composition of the Bible does not refute the doctrine of inerrancy.

While the human authorship of Scripture cannot be ignored, neither can the divine side. God spoke through these writers.

It also must be noted that the authors of Scripture, as well as the prophets who did not write, were only infallible or inerrant in what they wrote or said when directed by the Lord—they were not inerrant in everything that they did. The example of Nathan the prophet shows that this is the case.

Don't The Missing Autographs Disprove Inerrancy?

Since the original, or the autograph, of each biblical book has been lost, it is wrong to argue for an inerrant original that no longer exists. How can the Christian church assert the Bible is inerrant if it does not have the original writings? How can a person claim inerrancy for a book that no longer exists? Isn't this an absurd and irrational position?

A number of comments need to be made.

INERRANCY IS NOT AN IRRATIONAL BELIEF

The position of inerrancy, with respect to this question, is neither irrational nor is it absurd. The fact that there was an original of every book of the Bible goes without saying. The copies were made from something!

THERE IS NOT CONSTANT APPEAL TO SOME LOST ORIGINAL

In addition, we do not have to appeal to the lost original manuscripts in order to hold the doctrine of inerrancy. The number of places where there are scribal discrepancies in the text are few and have plausible solutions. It is not the case that the Christian has to continually appeal to some "lost original" to solve the problems discovered in the text, or to argue for an inerrant Scripture.

In fact, rarely, if ever, is the reading of the text the issue as to whether or not there is an error in Scripture. Difficulties are dealt with as the text *presently* stands in Scripture—they are not put aside and attributed to "textual corruptions." Scribal error is appealed to only when the evidence warrants it. It is not used as a convenient device to explain away difficulties.

Basically, the only time scribal error is considered as a possible solution to a problem is in the area of numbers and proper names. Apart from these instances, it is rarely appealed to. Thus, the doctrine of inerrancy is concerned with the Bible as we now possess it.

NO ONE HAS EVER SEEN AN ERRANT ORIGINAL

While we have not seen inerrant originals, we have not seen errant ones either. In addition, the church has never seen the risen Christ, but still believes in Him. Simon Peter wrote of Jesus Christ:

> Although you have not seen him, you love him; and even though you do not see him now, you believe in him and rejoice with an indescribable and glorious joy for you are receiving the outcome of your faith, the salvation of your souls (1 Peter 1:8,9 NRSV).

We love Jesus and believe Him to be the Savior based upon the best evidence. The same holds true for an inerrant Bible. We base our belief not on blind faith, but upon the weight of the evidence. The idea that we cannot see an inerrant autograph should not destroy our faith in one.

A LESSON FROM JESUS ABOUT THE OLD TESTAMENT

We learn a lesson from Jesus. While the originals of the Old Testament were, most likely, not around in His day, that did not stop Him from trusting its contents. Jesus believed and taught that our present Old Testament is the infallible, inerrant, Word of God. We should do likewise.

Luke tells us that Jesus read from the scroll of the prophet Isaiah at a synagogue in Nazareth. When Jesus read from the Scripture, He said the following:

> Then he began to tell them, "Today this scripture has been fulfilled even as you heard it being read" (Luke 4:21 NET).

From Jesus' statement we learn at least two things. First, there is such a thing as an authoritative Scripture.

Second, this Scripture has made predictions that have come true. Yet, the portion of Scripture from which Jesus read was not the original writing of Isaiah the prophet, but rather a copy of the original. Yet Jesus assumed this copy was authoritative Scripture.

LESSONS FROM OTHER NEW TESTAMENT CHARACTERS

We also learn the same lesson from other New Testament characters. Paul read from the Scripture in the city of Thessalonica. The Book of Acts explains it as follows:

> Paul went to the Jews in the synagogue, as he customarily did, and on three Sabbath days he addressed them from the scriptures, explaining and demonstrating that the Christ had to suffer and to rise from the dead, saying, "This Jesus I am proclaiming to you is the Christ" (Acts 17:2,3 NET).

This assumes that there was such a thing a group of writings called "Scripture."

In addition, the Bible says that Philip heard the Ethiopian eunuch reading Scripture. The Book of Acts records it as follows:

> Now the passage of the Scripture that he was reading was this: "Like a sheep he was led to the slaughter and like a lamb before its shearer is silent, so he opens not his mouth. In his

humiliation justice was denied him. Who can describe his generation? For his life is taken away from the earth" (Acts 8:32-33 ESV).

In each of these instances the Bible says they were reading portions of Scripture. However, they were not reading the autographs—they were reading copies of copies of the original. These copies contained scribal errors. Yet these copies of Scripture were considered to be divinely authoritative by Jesus and the other New Testament characters. They considered these Scripture portions to be the very Word of God. We should do likewise.

Therefore, the missing autograph's argument is not one that should be used against the idea of an inerrant Bible.

SUMMARY TO QUESTION 24
DON'T THE MISSING AUTOGRAPHS OF SCRIPTURE DISPROVE INERRANCY?

As far as we know, all the original writings of Scripture have long since vanished. Thus, we are dependent upon copies to reconstruct the text. The fact that the originals do not exist is a popular argument used against inerrancy. How can there be an inerrant Bible without any originals— particularly when there are scribal errors in the manuscripts that still exist?

This argument does not carry much weight. The fact that there were originals to each biblical book is beyond all doubt—the copies were made from something. In addition, the appeal is not often made to some "lost" original to hold to the doctrine of inerrancy. The present copies give us sufficient reason to trust its contents.

We also learn a lesson from Jesus. He had the present Old Testament that we have—without the originals. Yet He trusted it completely, and so should we.

The inerrancy of Scripture is not based upon any missing autograph—it is based upon what the Bible says about itself. It is God's Word, and God does not make mistakes.

Add to this is the reliable way in which the Scriptures have been transmitted. There is no evidence that any part of Scripture has been changed or tampered with.

What About The Mistakes In The Various Copies Of The Bible?

The mistakes in the different copies of the biblical manuscripts have also been used as an argument against inerrancy. Since there are mistakes in the copies it is wrong to assert inerrancy. How can one claim an inerrant original if all of the copies have errors? The following points need to be made about this issue.

MISTAKES WERE MADE IN COPYING SCRIPTURE

To begin with, we do admit that mistakes were made in copying. We can cite a few examples.

HOW OLD WAS AHAZIAH?

We find a discrepancy when we compare what the Bible says about the age of Ahaziah when he became king. We read the following in the Book of Second Kings:

> Ahaziah was twenty-two years old when he became king and he reigned for one year in Jerusalem. His mother was Athaliah, the granddaughter of King Omri of Israel (2 Kings 8:26 NIV).

According to Second Kings, Ahaziah was twenty-two when he became king. However, his age is given at forty-two in Chronicles. It says:

> Forty and two years old was Ahaziah when he began to reign, and he reigned one year in Jerusalem. His mother's name also was Athaliah the daughter of Omri (2 Chronicles 22:2 KJV).

Which of these is correct? Was he twenty-two or forty-two when he began to reign?

It should be noted that the Septuagint, the Greek translation of the Hebrew Old Testament, as well as certain Syriac manuscripts, read twenty-two here in Chronicles while the traditional Hebrew text says forty-two. This would make the text in Chronicles agree with the text in Kings.

A number of English translations follow the Septuagint and translate it as twenty-two. For example, the New International Version says:

> Ahaziah was twenty-two years old when he became king, and he reigned in Jerusalem one year. His mother's name was Athaliah, a granddaughter of Omri. (2 Chronicles 22:2 NIV).

Thus, there is no contradiction here if the New International Version has the correct reading.

HOW MANY STALLS FOR HORSES DID SOLOMON HAVE?

There are other examples. In Second Chronicles, the Bible says that Solomon had four thousand stalls for his horses. In Second Chronicles, we read:

> Solomon had four thousand stalls for his chariot horses and twelve thousand horses. He kept them in assigned cities and in Jerusalem (2 Chronicles 9:25 NIV).

However, in First Kings, it says Solomon had forty thousand stalls for his horses:

> And Solomon had forty thousand stalls of horses for his chariots, and twelve thousand horsemen (1 Kings 4:26 KJV).

The English Standard Version also reads forty thousand in the Book of First Kings:

> Solomon also had 40,000 stalls of horses for his chariots, and 12,000 horsemen (1 Kings 4:26 ESV).

However, some translations read "four thousand" in First Kings. An example of this is the New English Translation. It reads as follows:

> Solomon had four thousand stalls for his chariot horses and twelve thousand horses (1 Kings 4:26 NET).

They do this because some Greek manuscripts read four thousand. With this translation there is no problem.

OTHER PROBLEM PASSAGES

However, there are a number of discrepancies in some English translations where there is no obvious solution. What do we make of these problems? Are they genuine errors?

There are a couple of observations that need to be made.

COPIES ARE NOT THE SAME AS THE ORIGINAL

The solution to this question is simple. Copies of the various portions of Scripture are not the same as the original. A mistake in a copy is not the same as a mistake in the original.

Indeed, a mistake in a copy is a human mistake. If there was a mistake in the original, then it would have been God making that mistake. But God does not make mistakes. The Bible makes this very clear!

Therefore, any copy of Scripture is only authoritative to the extent that it accurately reproduces the original. Since we don't hold any human author responsible for mistakes in copies of an ordinary book, we should not hold God responsible for mistakes in copies of Scripture.

THE ERRORS DECREASE THE FURTHER WE GO BACK

Furthermore, as we get closer in time to the originals, the number of copyists' errors in the manuscripts decreases—they become fewer and fewer. Thus, most of the errors are able to be cleared up by closely examining the manuscript evidence. This is another reason that we should have trust in the text as it now stands.

THE TEXT IS IN GREAT SHAPE

The New Testament is also in great textual shape. The continuing work of New Testament textual criticism refines the present text. For all intents and purposes, the text of both testaments fairly represents the inerrant original.

WE KNOW WHERE THE TEXTUAL PROBLEMS ARE

Furthermore, we are aware where these variants reading are. In modern translations there are marginal notes that allow the reader to become aware of the various possible readings. In the margins there will be statements such as. "Some ancient authorities read," "other ancient manuscripts add" or "the oldest manuscripts read."

Consequently, the original is not lost.

THERE IS NO DOCTRINE OF SCRIPTURE OR ANY COMMAND THREATENED BY A VARIATION IN THE TEXT

It must be stressed that no doctrine of Scripture, nor any command to believers, is threatened by a variant reading. The manuscript variations do not materially affect the meaning of the text. Inerrancy is not affected by errors in copies copied from the original. This is not an issue.

THE GENERAL SENSE OF ANY PASSAGE OF SCRIPTURE IS CLEAR

In addition, the general sense of a passage is clear from the context. The variant readings do not really affect the overall context, or the basic sense of the passage. This is true for the entire Scripture. This is very important to keep in mind.

SHOULD WE EXPECT THERE TO BE NO MISTAKES IN SCRIPTURE?

It is argued that if God really wanted an inerrant Bible, then there would not have been any mistakes in the copies. The fact that the copies have demonstrable mistakes shows that an inerrant Bible was not something necessary in the plan of God. How do we respond to this objection?

THIS OBJECTION HAS NO MERIT

This objection has no basis in fact. First, it is not rational to think that God would supernaturally protect every scribe from error each and every time the text of Scripture was copied.

The New Testament alone has been copied hundreds of thousands of times. To assume that God would protect each scribe, every time they copied the text of Scripture, is not reasonable.

WE SHOULD NOT SPECULATE ABOUT WHAT GOD SHOULD HAVE DONE

In addition, we should be careful not to speculate about what we think God should have done or might have, done. No human being is in a position to do this. A person could also say that if God really cared about His Word, then He would not have allowed any false teachings to be brought into the church.

Yet He allowed false teaching to arise and warned believers about it. We simply do not know enough to say what God should have done. We are not God.

The Lord Himself has warned humanity about the limitations all of us have. He said:

> For my thoughts *are* not your thoughts, neither *are* your ways my ways, saith the LORD. For *as* the heavens are higher than the earth, so are my ways higher than your ways, and my thoughts than your thoughts (Isaiah 55:8,9 KJV).

We should not try to second guess God.

Consequently, the idea of an inerrant Bible is not refuted by mistakes in certain of the copies.

SUMMARY TO QUESTION 25
WHAT ABOUT THE MISTAKES IN THE VARIOUS COPIES OF THE BIBLICAL MANUSCRIPTS?

The various manuscript copies have errors in them. This has caused some to deny the doctrine of the inerrancy of Scripture. Yet no one claims that each manuscript was copied without errors being made. The only error-free documents were the originals.

While no one has ever denied that mistakes can be found into the various copies that have been made, this fact has nothing to do with the original.

Furthermore, the closer we get to the original wording of the text, we find that the errors become less and less.

In addition, the variant readings that do exist do not threaten any doctrine of Scripture, or any command that God gives to believers.

Moreover, the sense of any passage can be gathered from the immediate context—the variants in the manuscripts do not affect the overall content.

Consequently, there is every good reason to believe that the originals were error free.

Have The Discoveries Of Modern Science Shown That The Bible Contains Scientific Errors?

It is often claimed that modern science has rendered the idea of an inerrant Bible as something that is impossible. Indeed, we hear reports of the discovery of skulls of creatures who were half-human, half-ape which supposedly show that humans had a common ancestor with the ape. There are also the confident assertions that the theory of evolution has been proven beyond any doubt.

Indeed, we are told that every educated person is aware of this. Statements such as these have led some people to abandon the idea of an inerrant Bible because of the discoveries of modern science. They assume that the scientific statements found in the Bible are nothing but mythical ideas of a pre-scientific age. Do modern scientific findings refute the idea of an inerrant Scripture?

There are several responses to these charges.

SCIENCE IS NOT THE MAIN TOPIC OF SCRIPTURE

To begin with, the Bible is not a book that was primarily written to deal with subjects relating to science. Rather, it is God's revelation of Himself, and His plan, to the human race. Science and scientific issues are not the main topics.

When they are dealt with in Scripture it is always incidental to the main story. Scientific issues only occur when they have something to do with God's dealings with humanity. We never find scientific statements given merely for the purpose of teaching humanity something about science or nature.

Therefore, it is wrong to overemphasize the place of science in Scripture. The Bible is not trying to give us any detailed explanations of scientific matters.

THE BIBLE SPEAKS RELIABLY ABOUT SCIENCE

However, while the main interest in Scripture is not that of science and nature, whenever Scripture does speak on areas pertaining to science, it speaks reliably. God's character would not allow Himself to accurately reveal information about Himself on one level, the spiritual issues, but inaccurately reveal information in other areas—such as matters pertaining to science and nature. God is the God of truth—no matter what the subject.

Therefore, any statement that the Bible makes about science or nature will be accurate. Yet it will only be accurate to the degree that God is intending to teach us something about the nature of the universe. In other words, we should not try to read too much into some of the scientific statements, neither should we try to read too little into them. The key is to let the Scripture tell us what it is trying to teach us about science in any given context.

SCIENCE HAS NOT PROVEN ANY ERRORS IN SCRIPTURE

Contrary to the claims of some, scientific research has not proven anything that would refute Scripture. The theory of evolution, for example, is exactly that—a theory. The so-called "missing links" between humans and apes are not clear examples of some transitional creature between them. The missing links are still missing. Modern scientific discoveries have not refuted the teaching of Scripture.

THE BIBLE USES COMMON, OR NON-SCIENTIFIC, MODES OF EXPRESSION

There is something else that should be remembered. The Bible does not speak unscientifically—it speaks non-scientifically. The Bible uses common modes of expression such as the sun rising, and the sun standing still. In Joshua, we read of the sun rising:

> Until the LORD gives rest to your kindred as well as to you, and they too take possession of the land that the LORD your God is giving them. Then you shall return to your own land and take possession of it, the land that Moses the servant of the LORD gave you beyond the Jordan to the sunrise (Joshua 1:15 NIV).

However, we should note that the word translated "sunrise" can also be translated "east." The New English Translation says:

> Until the Lord gives your brothers a place like yours to settle and they conquer the land the Lord your God is ready to hand over to them. Then you may go back to your allotted land and occupy the land Moses the Lord's servant assigned you east of the Jordan" (Joshua 1:15 NET)

There is also the famous incident of the sun "standing still." We read about this in the Book of Joshua:

> So the sun stood still, and the moon stopped, until the nation avenged themselves of their enemies. (Joshua 10:13 NET).

These expressions were, and still are, the common ways of explaining things that are observable—they are not meant to be precise scientific statements. The technical term for this practice is phenomenal language.

Therefore, it is often said that the biblical writers spoke and wrote phenomenally. They describe things from the viewpoint of an observer.

They are not attempting to provide a scientific explanation of what is occurring.

THE BIBLE SPEAKS OF THINGS AS THEY APPEAR TO AN OBSERVER ON THE EARTH

In other words, Scripture speaks of things as they appear to an observer on the earth. If the Bible taught that things actually *appeared* a certain way to an observer, but they did not appear that way, then the Bible would be wrong.

Also, if the Bible taught that things *were* a certain way, such as the earth was indeed the center of the solar system, then the Bible would be in error.

However, if the Bible teaches that things *appear* a certain way, such as the sun rises and sets, this is not an error. Describing things as they appear is not the same as stating the way things actually are. All of us do this. The authors of Scripture should have the right to do the same.

CONCLUSION: THERE IS NO CONFLICT WHEN PROPERLY UNDERSTOOD

There is no conflict between science and Scripture when both are properly understood. The key is to understand exactly what the Bible says and what exactly science has proven. When this is done there will be no conflict between the two.

There have been some well-meaning Christians who have tried to make the Bible more precise than it attempts to be in the area of science. However, a proper interpretation of what science and the Scripture are saying will not try to say more than what the Bible is saying.

The issue is not trying to make the Bible conform to 21st century norms of scientific precision. The issue is: did the writers of Scripture speak accurately in what they were trying to convey to their readers? The answer is, "Yes."

SUMMARY TO QUESTION 26
HAVE THE DISCOVERIES OF MODERN SCIENCE SHOWN THAT THE BIBLE CONTAINS SCIENTIFIC ERRORS?

Modern science has supposedly made the doctrine of inerrancy obsolete. With the advent of the discoveries of modern science, the view of the world that was held in biblical times is now seen to have been wrong.

Yet this is not the case. Science and Scripture are not at odds with each other when there is a correct interpretation of what each of them are saying.

In sum, the Bible speaks non-scientifically. Yet what it does say matches up with scientific reality.

Why Don't The New Testament Writers Quote The Old Testament Word For Word?

One objection against the doctrine of the inerrancy of Scripture is the lack of word for word quoting of the Old Testament from the New Testament. This accusation can be summarized as follows.

ACCUSATION: LACK OF WORD FOR WORD QUOTING FROM THE OLD TESTAMENT REFUTES THE IDEA OF INERRANCY

If the Scripture teaches inerrancy, then why didn't the New Testament writers cite the Old Testament writers word for word? The lack of verbal exactness in citing the Old Testament has caused some to deny the biblical teaching of inerrancy.

RESPONSE

This objection does not carry much weight for a number of reasons. They include the following.

THERE ARE DIFFERENT LANGUAGES INVOLVED IN THE TWO TESTAMENTS

First, there is the issue of languages. The Old Testament was written in Hebrew, with parts in Aramaic, while the New Testament was composed in Greek. Any quotation, therefore, cannot be given word for word because there are two different languages involved. There had to be a translation from one language to another.

THE ANCIENT PRACTICE OF CITING ANOTHER WRITTEN WORK MUST BE APPRECIATED

While in some modern cultures it is the accepted method to quote another author word for word, this was not the case in biblical times. It is not so much the exact words, as the exact content that was being cited.

As long as the content is accurately stated, then it is not necessary to quote the author word for word. The Old Testament was not quoted for its words, but rather for the meaning. The New Testament writers also expanded upon what was written. They gave the true meaning as well as the application.

THIS MISTAKENLY ASSUMES THE WRITER MUST QUOTE ANOTHER WRITTEN SOURCE WORD FOR WORD

The attack is based on the assumption that citations must give the exact words of the writer quoted, when no such rule exists in literature. Unless the writer specifically says that he is quoting another word for word, we should not assume that this is the case. Writers are quoting correctly if they give the true sense of the text.

THERE WAS A FREE MANNER OF QUOTING THE OLD TESTAMENT

The New Testament writers frequently quote the Old Testament without verbal exactness. Most likely, many of the quotations were from memory. At times, the citations were made according to the sense of the Old Testament passage rather than making a direct quote from the passage.

THE QUOTATIONS ARE SOMETIMES INDIRECT

Sometimes the quotations in Scripture are indirect, not direct. An indirect quotation does not cite someone directly but does report accurately what that person said.

For example, John makes the statement to us, "I was at work from nine in the morning until five in the evening." Then we, in turn, tell someone that John told us that he was at work all day. While our sentence does not quote John word for word, it does give an accurate account of what he said.

Although an indirect quotation may not use any of the speaker's original words, it can correctly report what the speaker said. The point is that indirect citing of someone can be accurate without using someone's exact words.

THERE WERE NO PUNCTUATION MARKS IN THE ORIGINAL

Another thing that needs to be emphasized is that the ancients did not use the same type of punctuation as we do today. There were no punctuation marks, ellipses, brackets, or other such devices in the original writings of Scripture—the autographs.

Consequently, we do not know whether the ancient writer was citing something directly or alluding to it.

Therefore, in some instances, the so-called "misquotation" is not a citation of Scripture at all. There was no intent of the writer to cite another portion of Scripture.

There are several other points that need to be emphasized.

THERE IS ONE AUTHOR BEHIND ALL OF SCRIPTURE: THE HOLY SPIRIT

The Bible emphasizes that the Holy Spirit is author of the entire Bible. Peter wrote the following about the work of the Holy Spirit in the divine inspiration of Scripture:

> Above all, you must understand that no prophecy of Scripture came about by the prophet's own interpretation. For prophecy never had its origin in the will of man, but

men spoke from God as they were carried along by the Holy Spirit (2 Peter 1:20-21 NIV).

Since this is the case, we should allow the author of the Old Testament—God the Holy Spirit—to quote Himself as He pleases.

THIS THEORY ASSUMES THE APOSTLES WERE IGNORANT OF SCRIPTURE

The attack is also based on the assumption that the apostles, when judged by modern standards, were rather ignorant in the area of theology. This is a rather arrogant position to hold—seeing that they were two thousand years closer to the Old Testament than we now are, and consequently were in a much better position to evaluate the evidence and to cite it correctly.

THERE IS HARDLY EVER ANY ATTEMPT TO HARMONIZE

Whenever there is a seeming problem with the way a New Testament writer quotes the Old Testament, an error is automatically assumed—no attempt is made to find a solution. This is not a fair way to deal with the issue.

INERRANCY ONLY REQUIRES THAT THE BIBLE ALWAYS TELLS THE TRUTH

Inerrancy does not require word for word quotations from the Old Testament by the New Testament writers. The doctrine of inerrancy simply means that the Bible always tells the truth. Time and time again we find the writers doing this.

SUMMARY TO QUESTION 27
WHY DON'T THE NEW TESTAMENT WRITERS QUOTE THE OLD TESTAMENT WORD FOR WORD?

One of the main objections against an inerrant Bible is the lack of verbal exactness when the New Testament quotes the Old. The fact that the Old Testament passage is not quoted word for word supposedly is an argument against the doctrine of inerrancy.

However, this is not the case. First, the Old Testament was written in Hebrew while the New Testament was composed in Greek. This makes verbal exactness impossible.

In addition, in ancient writing there were no such things as punctuation marks, quotation marks, or any other such devices.

Consequently, one can never be certain when a passage is being directly cited, or merely paraphrased.

It also may be asked, "Why must an author quote another word for word to be faithful to what the quoted author wrote?"

It must be remembered that the Holy Spirit is the ultimate author behind all the books of Scripture. Should He not be able to quote His own work any way that He wishes?

Finally, the biblical doctrine of inerrancy does not demand the Old Testament be quoted word for word in the New Testament. The doctrine of inerrancy requires that the Bible should always tell the truth. This is exactly what it does.

QUESTION 28

Does Inerrancy Cause Worship
Of The Bible? (Bibliolatry)

Some have objected to the doctrine of inerrancy because it supposedly makes people worship the Bible rather than the God who is behind the writing of the Bible. This worship of the Bible is known as "bibliolatry."

DO CHRISTIANS WORSHIP AN INERRANT BIBLE?

The idea is that people will make the Bible the object of their worship if they believe it to be an inerrant, or infallible, document. Instead of worshipping the God of Scripture, people will worship the very Scripture itself. This approach has a number of weaknesses.

WOULD AN ERRANT BIBLE CAUSE A GREATER DESIRE TO WORSHIP GOD?

First, are we to assume that an untrustworthy, errant Bible would cause a person to have a greater desire to trust God? Would this give assurance that God and His Word could always be relied upon? Obviously, it would not.

THE BIBLE DOES NOT TEACH WORSHIP OF ITSELF

Add to this, the Bible itself does not contain any passage that would remotely give one the idea to worship it rather than God. To the contrary, Scripture makes it clear that God, and He alone, should be worshipped. In the Ten Commandments we read:

> You shall not make for yourself an idol, or any likeness of what is in heaven above or on the earth beneath, or in the water under the earth. You shall not worship them nor serve them; for I, the LORD your God, am a jealous God, inflicting the punishment of the fathers on the children, on the third and the fourth generations of those who hate Me (Exodus 20:4,5 NASB 2020).

God forbids worship of anything apart from Himself—this includes His written Word.

WE CANNOT BLAME SCRIPTURE FOR THE SINS OF HUMANS

While there are people who do have a superstitious attitude toward the Bible, they do not get this idea from a reading of the Scripture. The Bible cannot be blamed for their faults.

Christians do not worship the Bible. Rather, it is the authoritative standard that God uses to make known His truth to humanity. It is the God of the Bible whom we willingly worship.

SUMMARY TO QUESTION 28
DOES INERRANCY CAUSE WORSHIP OF THE BIBLE? (BIBLIOLATRY)

The doctrine of inerrancy supposedly makes a person worship the Bible instead of God. This, it is contended, should cause the idea of inerrancy to be abandoned.

While some may place a superstitious attitude toward the writings of Scripture, this has nothing to do with the issue of inerrancy.

The Bible does not encourage worship of itself—it always points to the worship of the living God. The belief in inerrancy should not be abandoned because some people mistakenly worship the Book instead of the God who divinely inspired the Book.

QUESTION 29

Aren't There Too Many Qualifications To The Definition Of Inerrancy?

Supposedly those who believe in inerrancy have so many qualifications to their definition that they make it theoretically impossible to prove an error in Scripture. Every time a supposed error is found, those who believe in inerrancy redefine inerrancy in such a way that it makes proving an error impossible. The doctrine of inerrancy is therefore meaningless.

Those who believe in inerrancy reject this idea. A number of points need to be emphasized in response.

THE PROBLEMS IN SCRIPTURE ARE NOT IGNORED

Those who believe in the doctrine of inerrancy realize that there are problems involved in the text as it presently stands. They do their best to come up with workable solutions. These scholars do not ignore the problems, neither do they define them out of existence.

Instead they work hard to try to find a reasonable answer to the difficulty. While in the past some Bible believers may have given simplistic answers to difficult problems, this is no longer true today.

THOSE WHO BELIEVE IN INERRANCY RECOGNIZE WHAT AN ERROR CONSISTS OF

Although some writers may be guilty of defining biblical inerrancy in such a way that it is meaningless, this is not the case with most Bible scholars who believe in inerrancy. It is important to recognize that those who accept the doctrine of inerrancy realize what an actual error is, and what it is not. They do not create some impossible standard that could never be met.

It is realized that there are a number of things that would actually constitute an error.

First, an error can be a misstatement of fact. For example, it could be attributing something to someone that was not true such as claiming Pontius Pilate was actually a Jewish leader, or that King Herod eventually became the Roman Caesar. If the Bible made claims like this, then it would constitute an error.

Contradictory statements between two authors, or in the writings of one author, would also constitute an error. If an author clearly contradicts what he has written elsewhere, or contradicts another biblical author, this would make the Scripture in error.

Therefore, those who believe in inerrancy realize for the doctrine to be meaningful there must be a realistic understanding of what an error consists of.

APPEAL IS NOT ALWAYS MADE TO SOME LOST ORIGINAL WHEN A PROBLEM ARISES

One of the accusations that seemingly makes the doctrine of inerrancy meaningless is the appeal to "lost originals." When an obvious mistake in Scripture is found, it is explained away by suggesting the error is only in the copies, but not the original. It is charged that doing this makes the doctrine of inerrancy meaningless.

However, it is not true that Christians often resort to saying that the mistake is in the copy, not the original. The difficulty needs to be worked out with the text that is now available—not the continuous appeal to some lost original. Those who believe in inerrancy understand this and work with the text as it stands.

Appealing to a lost original should only be done in the smallest number of cases and only when the original reading is uncertain.

IT IS RECOGNIZED THAT SOME PROBLEMS DO NOT HAVE IMMEDIATE SOLUTIONS

That there are problems that do not have an immediate solution is recognized by Bible-believers. The people who have faith in the living God and His Word wait for further information to deal with problems where there is presently no solution. They make the distinction between a difficulty and a proven error. A difficulty is a problem for which there is no answer at the time.

An error is a proven contradiction. While there are indeed a number of difficulties associated with Scripture, there still has yet to be a proven error.

INERRANCY IS A BIBLICAL BELIEF

Those who advocate inerrancy start with the belief that the Bible has about itself—it is true in everything that it says. With that as a starting point, they tackle the problems they confront in Scripture—they do not attempt to define the problem out of existence or refuse to acknowledge that difficult areas do indeed exist. Rather they take the perspective that the words of the Bible ultimately derive from a perfect God who cannot lie.

SUMMARY TO QUESTION 29 AREN'T THERE TOO MANY QUALIFICATIONS TO THE DEFINITION OF INERRANCY?

Critics charge that individuals who hold to the doctrine of inerrancy make too many qualifications to allow the idea to be meaningful. Every time an error in Scripture is demonstrated, the doctrine of inerrancy is supposedly redefined so as to make the error go away.

While there may be some who do this, there are responsible biblical scholars who face the Bible difficulties. They neither ignore them, nor qualify them in such a way as to remove the supposed error.

It again must be emphasized that a difficulty is not the same thing as an error. If there is a plausible solution to a certain difficulty, then it is wrong to call it an error.

QUESTION 30

Are Many Statements Of Scripture Outside The Realm Of Being Inerrant?

One curious argument against biblical inerrancy makes the observation that not all statements in Scripture can be proven true or false.

For example, commands such as, "Pray without ceasing" or "Trust in the Lord with all your heart" cannot be said to be either true or false because they are not assertions of fact.

In addition, there are those portions of Scripture where the writer worships the Lord with adoring praise. These statements cannot be said to be either true or false.

Therefore, many statements in Scripture are outside of the realm of being errant, or inerrant. Since this is the case, how can one say that all the words of the Bible are inerrant?

IT IS RECOGNIZED THAT NOT EVERY STATEMENT FOUND IN SCRIPTURE CAN BE FALSIFIED

This objection does not understand the doctrine of inerrancy. Inerrancy merely holds that those statements in Scripture that can be proven to be true or false are always true. It does not hold that every statement in the Bible can be falsified. No one argues that every statement made in Scripture can be proven true or false.

Inerrancy asserts that all the words of Scripture are accurately reported. In addition, the statements made by God, or by one of His prophets when they are speaking for God, are without errors.

In Scripture, we find a number of statements that assert facts or truth. However, not all of these statements can be independently verified. We can categorize these statements as follows.

THERE ARE MANY STATEMENTS THAT CAN BE HISTORICALLY VERIFIED

The Bible contains a number of statements which can be independently verified as true or false. For example, we read the following in Luke's gospel:

> Now in the fifteenth year of the reign of Tiberius Caesar, Pontius Pilate being governor of Judea, Herod being tetrarch of Galilee, his brother Philip tetrarch of Iturea and the region of Trachonitis, and Lysanias tetrarch of Abilene, while Annas and Caiaphas were high priests, the word of God came to John the son of Zacharias in the wilderness (Luke 3:1,2 NKJV).

Luke mentions seven historical figures that lived and ruled together at a set time in history—the fifteenth year of Tiberius Caesar. This statement can be examined to determine whether or not it matches up with historical characters that were known to live. It does.

THERE ARE EXPLANATIONS OF THE MEANING OF THE HISTORICAL FACTS

There are other statements of fact that are found in Scripture that cannot be verified by any type of historical investigation.

For example, the Bible says that Jesus Christ was crucified in the city of Jerusalem. It also says that He was buried, rose from the dead, and appeared alive after His death.

It is possible that historical investigation can determine whether or not this really occurred. However, historical investigation cannot determine the significance or meaning of the death of Christ. Paul wrote the following to the Corinthians:

> For I delivered to you first of all that which I also received: that Christ died for our sins according to the Scriptures, and that He was buried, and that He rose again the third day according to the Scriptures, and that He was seen by Cephas, then by the twelve (1 Corinthians 15:3-5 NKJV).

The New Century Version translates the verses in this manner.

> I passed on to you what I received, of which this was most important: that Christ died for our sins, as the Scriptures say; that he was buried and was raised to life on the third day as the Scriptures say and that he was seen by Peter and then by the twelve apostles (1 Corinthians 15:3-5 NCV).

Historical investigation cannot tell us the meaning of His death.

Therefore, the statement of Paul "that Christ died for our sins according to the Scriptures" is totally trustworthy, but it is outside the realm of any sort of historical investigation.

SCRIPTURE CONTAINS PERSONAL TESTIMONIES TO GOD'S GOODNESS

There are a number of statements in Scripture that could be placed under the category of personal testimonies. These statements testify to the goodness and faithfulness of God.

FOR EXAMPLE, WE READ THE FOLLOWING IN THE BOOK OF PSALMS:

> Happy are those whose way is blameless, who walk in the law of the LORD. Happy are those who keep his decrees, who seek him with their whole heart, who also do no wrong, but walk in his ways (Psalm 119:1-3 NRSV).

Here is a general statement that those who obey God's law are happy or blessed.

Again, while these statements are trustworthy, they cannot be independently verified as either true or false in the same way a statement of historical fact can be verified.

Therefore, we must appreciate that the Bible contains a number of statements that cannot, in the historical sense, be proven to be true or false. Hence the term "inerrancy" would not apply to them.

THE BIBLE IS TOTALLY TRUSTWORTHY IN ALL THAT IT SAYS: THIS IS THE DOCTRINE OF INERRANCY

This is why it is important to go beyond the term inerrancy when describing the nature of statements found in the Bible. Inerrancy, while true, is a limited concept—more needs to be said about the nature of the Bible than it is merely without error.

What must be emphasized is that the Bible is totally trustworthy in all that it says. This covers all statements that are found in Scripture. This includes verifiable facts or spiritual principles that are laid down—everything is true.

SUMMARY TO QUESTION 30
AREN'T MANY STATEMENTS OF THE SCRIPTURE OUTSIDE THE REALM OF BEING INERRANT?

The idea of inerrancy is irrelevant for much of Scripture because many statements do not fall into the category of being proven true or false.

However, those who hold to the doctrine of inerrancy recognize this. Inerrancy states that those parts of Scripture that fall under the category of being proven true or false will always be found to be correct. It does not mean that every statement of Scripture can be proven true or false.

Statements that explain why a certain event happened cannot be proven to be true or false by normal historical investigation. Neither can statements that personally testify to God's goodness for those who trust Him. Yet these statements are true.

This is why the term inerrancy is limited in its scope. The emphasis on the nature of the Bible should be that it is totally trustworthy in all that it says. This includes those types of statements where the historical method cannot determine whether they are true or false.

Since All Bible Translations Are Imperfect How Can We Speak Of An Inerrant Bible?

It is objected that the Scripture today cannot be called inerrant because each translation made from the original is imperfect. Indeed, no matter what language the Bible is translated into, there will always be imperfections.

How, therefore, can the Bible today be spoken of as the inerrant Word of God when most people read it in an imperfect translation?

RESPONSE

We respond to this accusation with the following points.

THE MESSAGE COMES THROUGH IN TRANSLATIONS

Admittedly there is no translation of Scripture that is perfect. Each has its deficiencies. Those who translate the Scripture recognize this. Yet the meaning of the passages can be adequately communicated from one language to the next.

For example, a simple comparison of good English translations of Scripture will demonstrate that the meanings of each passage will be shown to be the same, even if the wording is different. The message of Scripture comes out crystal clear.

TRANSLATIONS HAVE MORE THINGS RIGHT THAN WRONG

With respect to the major Bible translations that have been produced, there is much more right with them than things that are wrong. The things that are wrong are usually insignificant and they do not affect the central message.

Consequently, people can read these translations with the confidence they are reading the Word of God.

A LESSON FROM THE NEW TESTAMENT AND THE SEPTUAGINT

An example of how an imperfect translation can still be the inerrant Word of God is found in the usage that the New Testament writers make of the of the Septuagint—the Greek translation of the Hebrew Old Testament.

The New Testament quotes the Septuagint about one hundred and sixty specific times. Thirteen of those times, when quoting the Old Testament, the New Testament writers call the Septuagint, Scripture. This shows that the Septuagint, an imperfect Greek translation of the Hebrew original, is still considered to be Holy Scripture.

These quotations are as follows.

MATTHEW 21:42

Jesus cites the Septuagint when speaking of His predicted rejection by His own people—the Jews. We read in Matthew:

> Jesus said to them, "Have you never read in the Scriptures: 'The stone which the builders rejected has become the chief cornerstone. This was the LORD's doing, And it is marvelous in our eyes?" (Matthew 21:42 NKJV).

This cites Psalm 117:22-23 in the Septuagint. It is Psalm 118:22-23 in English translations. Jesus believed the Septuagint could be equated with Scripture.

LUKE 4:18-19,21

The Septuagint was cited by Jesus when He read from the scroll of Isaiah in a synagogue in Nazareth. It reads as follows:

> Now Jesus came to Nazareth, where he had been brought up, and went into the synagogue on the Sabbath day, as was his custom. He stood up to read, and the scroll of the prophet Isaiah was given to him. He unrolled the scroll and found the place where it was written, "The Spirit of the Lord is on me, because he has anointed me to proclaim good news to the poor. He has sent me to proclaim release to the captives and the regaining of sight to the blind, to set free those who are oppressed, to proclaim the year of the Lord's favor." Then he rolled up the scroll, gave it back to the attendant, and sat down. The eyes of everyone in the synagogue were fixed on him. Then he began to tell them, "Today this scripture has been fulfilled even as you heard it being read" (Luke 4:16-21 NET).

Jesus is citing Isaiah 61:1,2. He called the passage from which He read "Scripture." Again, the Septuagint is considered to be Scripture

JOHN 13:18

When Jesus said the Scriptures predicted His betrayal by one who was close to Him, the Lord cited the Septuagint. We read the following in the Gospel of John:

> I do not speak concerning all of you. I know whom I have chosen; but that the Scripture may be fulfilled, 'He who eats bread with Me has lifted up his heel against Me' (John 13:18 NKJV).

This cites Psalm 40:9 in the Septuagint (Psalm 41:9 in English translations). The Greek text of the Old Testament is cited here and it is declared to be Scripture.

ACTS 8:32-33

When leaving Jerusalem, the Ethiopian eunuch was reading the Septuagint translation of the Old Testament about the prediction of God's suffering servant. The Bible records it as follows:

> Now the passage of the scripture that he was reading was this: "Like a sheep he was led to the slaughter, and like a lamb silent before its shearer, so he does not open his mouth. In his humiliation justice was denied him. Who can describe his generation? For his life is taken away from the earth" (Acts 8:32-33 NRSV).

This is citing Isaiah 53:7,8 in the Septuagint.

ROMANS 4:3

Paul quotes the Septuagint when referring to the faith of Abraham. He said to the Romans:

> For the Scriptures tell us, "Abraham believed God, so God declared him to be righteous" (Romans 4:3 NLT).

The passage cited is Genesis 15:6 and it is called Scripture.

ROMANS 9:17

Paul cites the Septuagint when speaking of God's reason for the raising up the Pharaoh of Egypt. He wrote to the church at Rome:

> For the Scripture says to Pharaoh, "For this very purpose I have raised you up, that I might show my power in you, and that my name might be proclaimed in all the earth" (Romans 9:17 ESV).

The New Living Translation says:

> For the Scriptures say that God told Pharaoh, "I have appointed you for the very purpose of displaying my power in you, and so that my fame might spread throughout the earth" (Romans 9:17 NLT).

Paul is citing Exodus 9:16 in the Septuagint and calls it Scripture.

ROMANS 11:3,4

The Septuagint is cited when referring to Elijah's complaint that all the prophets had been slain. We read the following in the Book of Romans:

> I ask, then, has God rejected his people? By no means! For I myself am an Israelite, a descendant of Abraham, a member of the tribe of Benjamin. God has not rejected his people whom he foreknew. Do you not know what the Scripture says of Elijah, how he appeals to God against Israel? "Lord, they have killed your prophets, they have demolished your altars, and I alone am left, and they seek my life." But what is God's reply to him? "I have kept for myself seven thousand men who have not bowed the knee to Baal" (Romans 11:2-4 ESV).

Here Paul is citing 1 Kings 19:10,14, and 18 in the Septuagint translation.

GALATIANS 3:8

Paul quotes the Septuagint in the passage that says Gentiles would be blessed through Abraham. He wrote the following:

> And the scripture, foreseeing that God would justify the Gentiles by faith, declared the gospel beforehand to Abraham, saying, "All the Gentiles shall be blessed in you" (Galatians 3:8 NRSV).

The passage cited is Genesis 12:3. Paul cites the Greek text rather than the Hebrew text.

GALATIANS 4:30

The illustration that the promise of the inheritance will come through Sarah, rather than Hagar, is quoted in the Septuagint. Paul wrote:

> But what does the Scripture say? "Get rid of the slave woman and her son, for the slave woman's son will never share in the inheritance with the free woman's son" (Galatians 4:30 TNIV).

Here Paul is citing Genesis 21:12 in the Greek text.

1 TIMOTHY 5:18

Paul quotes the Law of Moses in the Septuagint version. He wrote the following to Timothy:

> For the scripture says, "You shall not muzzle an ox while it is treading out the grain," and, "The laborer deserves to be paid" (1 Timothy 5:18 NRSV)

Deuteronomy 25:4 is cited here in the Greek text.

JAMES 2:8

James cites the Septuagint with respect to loving one's neighbor. He wrote:

> Yes indeed, it is good when you truly obey our Lord's royal command found in the Scriptures: "Love your neighbor as yourself" (James 2:8 NLT).

James is citing Leviticus 19:18 in the Greek translation of the Hebrew Old Testament.

JAMES 4:6

James quotes the Septuagint concerning God blessing the humble. He said:

> He gives us more and more strength to stand against such evil desires. As the Scriptures say, "God sets himself against the proud, but he shows favor to the humble" (James 4:6 NLT).

The passage cited here is Proverbs 3:34 in the Septuagint.

Each Of These References Calls What They Are Citing "Scripture"

We find the evidence convincing. On a number of occasions, the New Testament writers, in citing the Old Testament, cite the Greek text, the Septuagint, instead of citing the Hebrew text. The Septuagint is called "Scripture" in thirteen passages where it is cited.

CONCLUSION: THE NEW TESTAMENT WRITERS BELIEVED THEY WERE CITING SCRIPTURE WHEN QUOTING THE GREEK OLD TESTAMENT

Therefore, the New Testament teaches that the Septuagint, a Greek translation, is Scripture. Since all Scripture is divinely inspired, then the Septuagint, along with other Bible translations, is divinely inspired in the sense that it conveys God's truth.

SUMMARY TO QUESTION 31
SINCE ALL BIBLE TRANSLATIONS ARE IMPERFECT HOW CAN WE SPEAK OF AN INERRANT BIBLE?

The imperfections of Bible translations are used as an argument against an inerrant Bible. Since all translations are different, how can anyone speak of an inerrant Bible?

However, the problems with translations have nothing to do with the original. It is admitted that all translations have their problems.

Yet the message still comes through loud and clear. The real issue is the text behind the translations. Is it error free? The evidence says that it is.

In addition, the New Testament cites the Septuagint, a Greek translation of the Hebrew Old Testament, and calls it Scripture.

Therefore, it is a biblical idea to call a translation of the Bible "Scripture."

Did Jesus Believe The Scriptures Were Without Error?

It is important that we look at the way in which the Lord Jesus Christ regarded Scripture. Jesus not only claimed to be God the Son, He demonstrated that His claims were true.

Consequently, He speaks with final authority on every issue. Therefore, we should seek to discover His attitude toward the Scripture.

WHAT JESUS TAUGHT ABOUT SCRIPTURE

When we examine the way that Jesus viewed Scripture, we can see that He trusted it totally—He believed it to be without error. The following points need to be observed.

ALL SCRIPTURE WAS DIVINELY INSPIRED

Jesus believed that the Scripture, in its entirety, is God-breathed. When confronted with the temptation of the devil He said the following:

> It is written, 'Man shall not live by bread alone, but by every word that comes from the mouth of God' (Matthew 4:4 ESV).

Christ believed in the full authority of Scripture. Humans are to live by every word that comes from of the mouth of God. All parts, and every word, were considered important to Jesus. In another place, He said:

> Do not think that I have come to abolish the law or the prophets. I have not come to abolish but to fulfill. I tell you the truth, until heaven and earth pass away not the smallest letter or stroke of a letter will pass from the law until everything takes place (Matthew 5:17,18 NET).

Jesus accepted the totality of Scripture as being divinely inspired of God. No exceptions.

THE OLD TESTAMENT IS HISTORICALLY ACCURATE

Jesus spoke of the Old Testament in terms of actual history. He believed that the people mentioned actually existed and the events recorded truly occurred.

These include: Adam and Eve (Matthew 19), Jonah and the great sea monster (Matthew 12), and Noah and the Flood (Matthew 24). There is not the slightest hint that Jesus cast doubt on any of the stories contained in the Old Testament.

THE BIBLE IS A UNITY

Jesus also testified the Scriptures were a unity—one unfolding complete story. On the day of His resurrection, we read about what Jesus said to two of His disciples traveling with Him on the road to Emmaus:

> He said to them, "This is what I told you while I was still with you: Everything must be fulfilled that is written about me in the Law of Moses, the Prophets and the Psalms" (Luke 24:44 NIV).

Jesus said that the Scripture cannot be broken:

> If he called them gods, to whom the word of God came (and the Scripture cannot be nullified) (John 10:35 NASB 2020)

Christ said that the entire Old Testament witnesses to His Person and work. We read in Luke:

> Then beginning with Moses and all the prophets, he interpreted to them the things written about himself in all the scriptures (Luke 24:27 NET).

To Jesus, the Old Testament was a unity; all of it needed to be examined.

JESUS SAID THE SCRIPTURE MUST BE FULFILLED

Because the Bible is God's divinely inspired Word, everything that it says must be fulfilled. Jesus said to those who arrested Him:

> But how then should the Scriptures be fulfilled, that it must be so? (Matthew 26:54 ESV).

It was absolutely necessary for the Scripture to be fulfilled.

HE SAID GOD'S WORD IS TRUE

Jesus said that God's Word is also without error. John recorded Jesus praying the following to God the Father:

> Set them apart in the truth; your word is truth (John 17:17 NET).

Jesus accepted the truthfulness of God's Word.

THE SCRIPTURES ARE SUFFICIENT FOR SALVATION

The truth of the Scripture is sufficient for the salvation of the people. In the story Jesus told of the rich man and Lazarus, the Lord made it clear that the Scriptures contained sufficient information for a person to be saved:

> And he said unto him, If they hear not Moses and the prophets, neither will they be persuaded, though one rose from the dead (Luke 16:31 KJV).

The New English Translation translates it this way:

> He replied to him, 'If they do not respond to Moses and the prophets, they will not be convinced even if someone rises from the dead'" (Luke 16:31 NET).

According to Jesus, the Scripture provided enough information for a person to make a decision for or against Christ.

JESUS APPEALED TO SCRIPTURE TO DEFEND HIS ACTIONS

We find that Jesus appealed to Scripture to defend His actions. He said that His arrest was a fulfillment of Scripture:

> At that hour Jesus said to the crowds, "Have you come out with swords and clubs to arrest me as though I were a bandit? Day after day I sat in the temple teaching, and you did not arrest me. But all this has taken place, so that the scriptures of the prophets may be fulfilled." Then all the disciples deserted him and fled (Matthew 26:55-56 NRSV).

When Jesus cleansed the temple, He appealed to Scripture to explain His actions. In Mark's gospel we read:

> Then they came to Jerusalem. Jesus entered the temple area and began to drive out those who were selling and buying in the temple courts. He turned over the tables of the moneychangers and the chairs of those selling doves, and he would not permit anyone to carry merchandise through the temple courts. Then he began to teach them and said, "Is it not written: 'My house will be called a house of prayer for all nations'? But you have turned it into a den of robbers!" (Mark 11:15-17 NET).

From these passages we can see that Jesus gave the Old Testament His full approval. It is clear from Jesus' statements that He believed the Scripture to be without error.

Therefore, it is clear that Jesus accepted the view that the Old Testament was without error. To Him, the Old Testament was authoritative, the God of the Old Testament was the living God, and the teaching contained in the Old Testament was the teaching of the living God. In other words, what the Scripture said, God said. This was Jesus' view.

THE IMPORTANCE OF JESUS' TESTIMONY

The testimony of Jesus is vital because the Bible pictures Him as representing for God the Father. Jesus exercised all the authority of God. God the Father validated Jesus as His own divine Son by the resurrection from the dead. Paul said:

> While God has overlooked the times of human ignorance, now he commands all people everywhere to repent, because he has fixed a day on which he will have the world judged in righteousness by a man whom he has appointed, and of this he has given assurance to all by raising him from the dead (Acts 17:30-31 NRSV).

Paul also wrote to the church at Rome that Jesus was appointed to be the Son of God in power by His resurrection from the dead:

> From Paul, a slave of Christ Jesus, called to be an apostle, set apart for the gospel of God. This gospel he promised beforehand through his prophets in the holy scriptures, concerning his Son who was a descendant of David with reference to the flesh, who was appointed the Son-of-God-in-power according to the Holy Spirit by the resurrection from the dead, Jesus Christ our Lord (Romans 1:1-4 NET).

Jesus said all authority in heaven and earth has been given to Him. Matthew's gospel closes with these words of Jesus:

> And Jesus came and spoke to them, saying, "All authority has been given to Me in heaven and on earth. Go therefore and

make disciples of all the nations, baptizing them in the name of the Father and of the Son and of the Holy Spirit, teaching them to observe all things that I have commanded you; and lo, I am with you always, even to the end of the age" Amen. (Matthew 28:18-20 NKJV).

These facts make Jesus' testimony absolutely crucial. Whatever He says is the final word.

JESUS AND TRUTH: HE IS THE STANDARD OF TRUTH

Jesus Christ declared that He is the truth. In one of His most famous statements, Jesus declared Himself to be "the truth:"

I am the way, the truth, and the life (John 14:6 KJV).

This claim meant far more than the fact that He was a truthful person. He declares Himself to be *the Truth* in the sense that He is standard of truth.

In the Book of Revelation, John called Him the faithful witness:

From John, to the seven churches that are in Asia: Grace and peace to you from "he who is," and who was, and who is coming, and from the seven spirits who are before his throne, and from Jesus Christ—the faithful witness, the firstborn from among the dead, the ruler over the kings of the earth. To the one who loves us and has set us free from our sins at the cost of his own blood (Revelation 1:4,5 NET).

John also wrote in the Book of Revelation that Jesus is the "faithful and true witness:"

To the angel of the church in Laodicea write the following: "This is the solemn pronouncement of the Amen, the faithful and true witness, the originator of God's creation" (Revelation 3:14 NET).

Jesus said that He had come into the world to testify to the truth:

> Therefore Pilate said to Him, "So You are a king?" Jesus answered, "You say correctly that I am a king. For this purpose I have been born, and for this I have come into the world: to testify to the truth. Everyone who is of the truth listens to My voice." (John 18:37 NASB 2020).

Jesus did not merely come to testify to the meaning of truth—He is truth. Therefore, whatever He says about any subject is the final word on that matter.

WE HAVE THREE CHOICES WITH RESPECT TO JESUS' TESTIMONY

Since Jesus demonstrated total trust in the Scriptures, we have three different ways in which we can look at the issue. He was either deceived, ignorant, or He was telling the truth.

1. JESUS WAS A DECEIVER

If Jesus knew the Scriptures contained errors but taught the people that they were error-free, then He was a deceiver. This would make Jesus guilty of lying.

Whatever His motive may have been, it would prove that we could neither trust Him, nor the Scriptures. However, there is no evidence that Jesus ever lied about anything.

2. JESUS WAS IGNORANT

If the Bible contains factual errors of which Jesus did not know about, then it affects the way we view Him. If He were ignorant of this fact, then it is possible that He was ignorant of other facts.

Logically, if the Bible is not inerrant and Jesus thought it was, then He cannot be the One whom He claimed to be—God the Son. If we cannot trust Him on this subject, then we cannot trust Him on any subject.

3. THE BIBLE IS INERRANT

The only alternative that fits the facts is that Jesus taught the inerrancy of the Bible because He knew it was true. As the Son of God and the risen Savior, Jesus has demonstrated that He has the authority to make such statements. His Word on the subject is final. If Jesus viewed the Scriptures as being error-free, then the Scriptures are error free. End of story.

CHRISTIANS SHOULD HAVE THE SAME VIEW ON INERRANCY AS JESUS

For the believer, the view of Jesus toward the Scripture is the Christian view. Thus, if Christians are to be consistent, they will approach the Bible in the same manner as our Lord—believing it to be error-free.

Any person who claims Jesus is their Lord, yet rejects His testimony about the nature of Scripture, is not submitting to His Lordship.

In fact, Jesus told believers to learn from Him. We read the following in Matthew:

> Take my yoke upon you, and learn from me; for I am gentle and humble in heart, and you will find rest for your souls (Matthew 11:29 NRSV).

In another place He said the following about Himself:

> You call me Teacher and Lord—and you are right, for that is what I am (John 13:13 NRSV).

This being the case, in what sense can we call Him Teacher and Lord if we do not adopt His view of Scripture?

Jesus also asked His followers the following question:

But why do you call Me 'Lord, Lord,' and do not do the things which I say? (Luke 6:46 NKJV).

This is a good question. Those who claim to follow Him as Lord should take seriously His view of Scripture. His attitude should be our attitude.

SUMMARY TO QUESTION 32
DID JESUS BELIEVE THE SCRIPTURES WERE WITHOUT ERROR?

The position of Jesus with respect to errors in the Bible is clear—He believed the Scripture was error-free.

This can be found in the fact that He considered every Word to be trustworthy, believed the entire Old Testament was historically accurate, taught that the Scriptures were a unity, argued that everything written must be fulfilled, and believed that it contained enough information sufficient for salvation.

He also quoted the Scriptures to defend His actions. Jesus Christ totally trusted the Scripture and so should we.

We cannot reject the attitude of Jesus without undermining His entire authority. Either He knew what He was talking about, or He did not. If He did not, then He was either a willful deceiver, or He was ignorant.

The only other choice is that the Bible is inerrant, like Jesus believed. This is the biblical position and this is where all the evidence leads us.

ABOUT THE AUTHOR

Don Stewart is a graduate of Biola University and Talbot Theological Seminary (with the highest honors).

Don is a best-selling and award-winning author having authored, or co-authored, over seventy books. This includes the best-selling *Answers to Tough Questions*, with Josh McDowell, as well as the award-winning book *Family Handbook of Christian Knowledge: The Bible*. His various writings have been translated into over thirty different languages and have sold over a million copies. His available books can be found on his website www.educatingourworld.com.

Don is now a full-time missionary with GoinChrist Ministries. His website educatingourworld.com provides free resources for those wanting to know what Christians believe, as well as why we believe. Currently there are 61 books on the site in PDF form, totaling about 13,000 pages of material while answering over 1,900 questions. Eventually we hope to record all the books, as well as translating the material in other languages.

Made in the USA
Columbia, SC
14 March 2022

57676158R00114